The Shun Lee

COOKBOOK

The Shun Lee

COOKBOOK

RECIPES FROM A
CHINESE RESTAURANT
DYNASTY

Michael Tong

AND ELAINE LOUIE

PHOTOGRAPHS BY ROGÉRIO VOLTAN

WM
WILLIAM MORROW
An Imprint of HarperCollinsPublishers

HarperCollins books may be purchased for educational, business, or sales promotional use. For information please write: Special Markets Department, HarperCollins Publishers, 10 East 53rd Street, New York, NY 10022.

FIRST EDITION

Designed by rlf design
Photographs by Rogério Voltan

Library of Congress Cataloging-in-Publication Data has been applied for.

ISBN: 978-0-06-085407-2
ISBN-10: 0-06-085407-3

07 08 09 10 11 ❖/TP 10 9 8 7 6 5 4 3 2 1

Contents

Introduction

AS I WALK THROUGH THE DINING ROOMS of my restaurants, Shun Lee Palace and Shun Lee West, I am often stopped by customers who regale me with stories of how the restaurants changed the way they enjoy Chinese food. They tell me about the first time they had Mu Shu Pork, or how, as children, they loved hearing the gong that accompanied the arrival of Beijing Duck, or that they learned to use chopsticks at our tables. I am delighted and proud to be a part of their lives.

My personal story is also the story of how the real cooking of the most important regional Chinese cuisines came to America. Over the decades, the New York City restaurants I worked in, and then owned, introduced American diners to authentic Chinese dishes that are now classics, found on Asian restaurant menus all over this country. Crispy Orange Beef, Lake Tung Ting Prawns, Crispy Sea Bass . . . they all originated at Shun Lee. In addition to creating these dishes, we also exposed the collective palate of New York diners to the complex Chinese seasonings that are now part of the American culinary landscape.

When I first came to the United States more than forty years ago, it wasn't difficult to find Chinese food, as long as you were satisfied with the elegant but restrained cooking of the province of Canton. Menus in the Chinatowns of San Francisco, Los Angeles, Boston, and Chicago were strictly limited to fare that restaurateurs believed would appeal to their American clientele. For example, shrimp with lobster sauce—with no lobster in sight—was on every menu. A number of dishes that seemed Chinese (to Americans) but were never served in my homeland were also offered up, including egg foo yung, chow mein, and barbecued spareribs. In China we barbecued entire pigs, not just the ribs!

If the first Chinese chefs in America came from Canton, the Communist takeover of the mainland in 1949 changed all that. Cooks on Chinese merchant vessels, unwilling to return to the changed political landscape, jumped ship in Manhattan and received political asylum. These cooks, who came from all over China, opened storefront restaurants, the first Chinese restaurants to offer non-Cantonese fare. These operations were far uptown near Harlem, where the rent was cheap. The décor may have been basic, with fake wood paneling and linoleum floors, but the food was something else again. A Chinese culinary revolution was taking place in uptown Manhattan—but the only people experiencing it were Columbia University students looking for great, cheap food and Chinese immigrants longing for an authentic taste of home.

I was one of those Chinese, starved for the kind of cooking I loved. I grew up in Shanghai, Taiwan, and Hong Kong, three entirely different cities with radically dissimilar cuisines. My palate was similar to that of the American who loves to eat fried chicken in Atlanta, grilled salmon in Seattle, and pastrami in New York. I came to the United States as an engineering student, first at the University of Southern California, and then at Oklahoma State University. During the summer breaks, I worked as a waiter. In 1964 I ended up in New York, where I had family.

My uncle invited me to eat at a restaurant called Shun Lee, way uptown on Broadway at 91st Street. Here were the dishes that my mother and grandmother cooked—recipes from all corners of China, but especially Shanghai and Sichuan. Shanghai was represented by dishes like the famous Lion's Head (pork and cabbage meatballs) and Sichuan by Slippery Chicken. There were also specialties of Beijing, like Bejing Duck. The food was spectacular. The chef was Tsung Ting Wang, who had been the chef for no less a personage than Harrison Tung, Chiang Kai-shek's ambassador to the United States. There was also a Shun Lee on Lexington Avenue at 23rd Street, an address as unfashionable as the uptown one.

I came to know Chef Wang quite well. One year later, he confided that he was about to open his own restaurant, which he planned to call Shun Lee Dynasty, in Manhattan's Midtown East, which would be quite a radical change from the neighborhoods of his employer's Shun Lee restaurants. He asked me to join him in the venture. It took me a while to make the decision to leave engineering and go into the restaurant business, but eventually I became the maître d' at Shun Lee Dynasty.

Chef Wang's mission was to share the delightfully seasoned food of Shanghai and Sichuan with New Yorkers, and Shun Lee Dynasty was probably the first upscale Chinese restaurant to offer these cuisines, so far removed from Cantonese cooking. Tough cuts of meat were "red-cooked"—simmered in a mahogany-red, spiced soy sauce braise until they fell off the bone. More tender bits of meat, poultry, and seafood weren't just stir-fried, but first "passed through oil," a technique where the food is first gently fried to give it a silky texture. New Yorkers were entranced by dishes that were enlivened by the exciting, aromatic flavor of Sichuan peppercorns and whole chili peppers.

At that time Grace Chu, the grande dame of Chinese cooking teachers, was ensconced at the China Institute in Manhattan, where her classes influenced an entire generation of cooks, both American and Asian. One day she brought in a friend of hers, a polite Southern gentleman who had an exotic appetite. He returned many times alone, and I served him such adventuresome fare for the time as mu shu pork, frog legs, and tripe, which he enjoyed heartily. I had no idea who he was until he handed me his credit card: Mr. Craig Claiborne. Mr. Claiborne, as the restaurant critic for the *New York Times,* was one of the most powerful men in the food business. When his *New York Times Restaurant Guide* came out, Shun Lee Dynasty received four stars, the highest rating. This endorsement legitimized Chinese cooking for New Yorkers, putting our restaurant at the same level as the bastions of French cuisine in town.

With our success, Chef Wang and I became partners. Soon we opened Shun Lee Palace on East 55th Street, followed by Hunam on Second Avenue. The latter restaurant brought yet another important Chinese cuisine to New York: the fiery food of the Hunan province. Like the Sichuan and Shanghai fare at the Shun Lee restaurants, the Hunanese food caused a sensation. Imagine being served shrimp with cilantro for the first time: shrimp in a piquant sauce of garlic, scallions, vinegar, hot bean sauce, and chili oil, showered with fresh cilantro. We then received our second *New York Times* four-star review, this time from Raymond Sokolov. These two four-star reviews put not only Shun Lee on the map, but also the foods of Sichuan and Hunan.

People returned for specialties such as Slippery Chicken (shredded chicken on a bed of spinach with a spicy sauce) and Lake Tung Ting Shrimp (shrimp and vegetables cloaked in a delicate sauce, covered with a lace netting of fried egg whites). When the clientele began demanding these dishes at other Chinese restaurants, our competitors (or colleagues, depending on your outlook) strove to meet our standards, and our recipes became part of the collective culinary consciousness. Over the years, I'd say that we've served around 10 million meals; my two restaurants serve 900 meals daily, plus about 400 take-out orders. And now, in *The Shun Lee Cookbook,* I am happy to share these distinctive recipes with you.

CHINESE COOKING AT HOME is different than cooking in a restaurant, where our ranges have extremely hot burners, our woks are seasoned from constant use, and our deep-fryers are at the ready. No matter. These recipes have been tested in home kitchens with generic equipment (a 24-inch Hotpoint electric stove) with the home cook in mind. You will learn the secrets to re-creating these dishes:

high-quality ingredients, professional techniques such as "passing through," and the unique combinations of seasonings that make authentic Chinese cooking an extraordinary culinary event.

The important thing to remember is that all cooking is a learning experience. Even professional cooks learn something new each day, improvising and experimenting as they create meals. If you are new to Chinese cooking, take plenty of time to prepare the ingredients before you start the actual cooking, enjoying the slicing and measuring and tasting. Don't try to cook an entire menu of Chinese dishes, when just one item and an easy side dish will suffice. As you build up your skills, work your way up to serving a meal in the true Chinese fashion, with many courses of dishes cooked in various methods, from fried to braised.

When people come to Shun Lee Palace or Shun Lee West, they have a distinctive dining experience, with a standard of excellent food that they cannot get anyplace else. There's no reason why cooks shouldn't be able to re-create this same level of dining at home. *Shun lee* means "smooth sailing." With this book by your side, you will be able to make the Chinese food you love with this same relaxed and confident attitude.

The Chinese Pantry

AMERICANS COOK WITH INGREDIENTS from all over the globe, so our supermarkets are now international in scope. Your market may even have specific sections for Japanese, Mexican, and Chinese ingredients.

When I think back to the limited range of Chinese groceries that were available when I came to the United States in the 1960s, the comparison with what can now be found at nearly every supermarket is amazing. Condiments like oyster sauce, black bean sauce, and of course soy sauce are easy to find today; sesame oil, hot chili paste, and five-spice powder are also commonplace. The produce section will usually have Asian vegetables like baby bok choy and napa cabbage, as well as wrappers for wontons and spring rolls. Big squares of tofu are available in firm, soft, and silken versions, packed in vacuum-sealed plastic boxes.

That being said, in order to re-create the rich, complex flavors of authentic Chinese cooking, you may have to search out an Asian grocery in your area, or an online purveyor, for some of the more esoteric ingredients. As the number of Asian immigrants has increased during the past few decades, so has the need for Asian groceries. You may be surprised to find a local Asian grocer nearby, and even more surprised at the range of ingredients for sale. This is where you will find red rice, preserved vegetable, and salted duck eggs, among other treasures.

In some cases substitutions are possible, and I have suggested them where appropriate. But cooking with unusual ingredients is fun, and I encourage you to go on an Asian grocery shopping spree. Many of these items will keep indefinitely, so stock up. If your pantry is well supplied with Chinese ingredients, you can cook Chinese dishes without having to run out for one specific key ingredient, such as hot bean paste.

When shopping for Chinese ingredients, know that because of translation and spelling problems, the labeling can be somewhat creative. Sometimes a paste is called a sauce, or vice versa, or the spelling is different from what you expect. For example, Fen Zheng Rou Seasoning is the same product as Ruey Fah Steam Powder. When in doubt, read the ingredients list on the label to double-check; some packages have helpful pictures to guide you.

Over the years, I have developed preferences for certain brands of condiments, just as some people prefer a specific mustard or ketchup. I include my recommendations here. This is not, by far, a complete list of Chinese ingredients. Use it as a glossary for the ingredients included in these recipes.

Produce

BABY BOK CHOY. The typical large bok choy is a Chinese favorite, but it can be bland and watery when cooked. Baby bok choy, however, which can be found at Asian groceries, farmers' markets, natural food stores, and some supermarkets, is sweet and tender.

CHILI PEPPERS. Small chili peppers, either red or green, provide spicy heat to dishes. Different peppers generate different amounts of heat; if you can't find the one called for, use the variety you can find and adjust the quantity to taste. Tiny Thai peppers are very hot; elongated serrano and smooth-skinned cayenne chilies have plenty of heat, too. Jalapeño is a good all-round chili pepper. Anaheim is a large chili that thinks it's a spicy bell pepper. Usually a recipe says to discard the ribs and seeds, because that is where the hottest part, the capsaicin, is concentrated. If you prefer your food spicy, leave the seeds and ribs in. When handling chilies, be sure to use care, as capsaicin can be very irritating. If you have sensitive skin, wear rubber gloves when handling them. In any case, after working with chilies, wash your hands well with soap and water to avoid passing the burning oils onto other more delicate parts of your body, such as your eyes.

CHINESE BROCCOLI. The Chinese variety of this vegetable is very leafy, with tiny white flowers, and has a slightly bitter flavor. Look for it at Chinese groceries. Broccolini, a new thin-stemmed kind of broccoli found in many supermarkets, is much milder but is a good substitute; or use broccoli rabe.

CILANTRO. Sometimes called coriander (although that also refers to the dried seed of the same plant, used as a spice) or Chinese parsley, this herb resembles flat-leaf parsley but has its own distinct flavor and fragrance. It is sometimes sold with the roots attached, a sure way to tell it from parsley. To store cilantro, snip an inch or so off the stems and stand them in a glass of water, just like a bouquet. Cover the cilantro with a plastic produce bag and refrigerate it; it will keep fresh for a few days.

GALANGAL. This relative of ginger is used as a flavoring in Southeast Asian curries. It looks like ginger, but with a paler, lighter skin. On its own, it has a somewhat medicinal taste; it must be combined with other seasonings to be palatable. Galangal is available at Asian and Indian groceries. If you can't find it, use a bit more ginger, with which it is almost always paired.

GINGER. The freshest ginger is firm and has shiny skin; avoid wrinkled ginger. To store it, wrap the ginger in aluminum foil and refrigerate it; it will keep for a week or so. There is a recent fashion for freezing ginger—it does not work.

LEMONGRASS. An aromatic plant with an enticing citrus fragrance and flavor, lemongrass is sold in stalks about 18 inches long. Only the inner bulb is used. To prepare the bulb, first trim off the base of the stalk. Chop off and discard the thin top of the stalk, where it meets the wider bulb area. Peel off the tough outer layer to reveal the tender, pale bulb—the bottom 6 to 8 inches of the stalk. Discard the outer layers. Use a sharp knife to chop the bulb as required.

LOTUS ROOT. At first glance, this tuber looks like an elongated potato with pointed ends. When cut crosswise, it reveals a pattern of moderately large holes, making a very interesting-looking addition to mixed vegetable dishes. Store uncut lotus root in a dark cool place as you would potatoes; cut lotus root should be placed in a plastic bag and refrigerated.

NAPA CABBAGE. Sometimes labeled "nappa cabbage," this delicately flavored, pale green cabbage is the most popular vegetable in northern China. It is essential for Pan-fried Pork Dumplings and Lion's Head. Napa cabbage is stout and barrel-shaped. You may also see elongated, smaller heads: this is celery cabbage, and as the flavor is very similar, it can be substituted. For either type, choose relatively heavy specimens with no brown discoloration.

TARO. This tuber is not the most attractive relative of the potato family, with its very dark, scaly skin. Once peeled, it reveals a beige flesh with purplish veins. Cooked, it adds a bit of pale lavender/purple color to desserts like Chilled Tapioca and Fresh Fruit Soup.

WATER CHESTNUTS. Most Western cooks know only canned water chestnuts. If there was ever an example of the superiority of fresh produce over canned, water chestnuts is it. Fresh water chestnuts are remarkably sweet and crunchy, while canned ones are bland. Peeling the dark brown skin of the fresh ones may seem tiresome (just get a sturdy paring knife and go to it), but the results are worth the effort. As you rarely need more than a few water chestnuts at a time, you won't be dedicating hours to the chore. But if you can't find fresh chestnuts, use the canned ones, well rinsed to help remove the tinned taste.

Canned

BAMBOO SHOOTS. The most familiar shoots come sliced and canned, but they can also be purchased whole or halved, plucked from buckets of water in the produce department at Asian grocery stores. To rid canned bamboo shoots of their tinny flavor, boil them in a saucepan of water for 1 minute, then drain and rinse well. If you don't have the time for this step, at the very least rinse them very well before using. (The bucket-stored shoots are processed as well, but they taste better than canned and need little preparation other than slicing.) Refrigerate any leftover bamboo shoots, covered with water in a covered container, changing the water every day or so; they will keep for up to 2 weeks. I recommend the Ma Ling and Companion brands.

COCONUT MILK. You can find canned unsweetened coconut milk in your supermarket or in Asian and Latin markets. Do not confuse it with sweetened cream of coconut, which usually goes by a brand name and is used for sweet cocktails, not cooking. And don't mistake it for the clear juice of a cracked coconut. Shake the can well before opening it, and refrigerate leftovers in a covered container for up to a week.

LOTUS PASTE. The canned sweetened paste made from lotus seeds has a chestnutlike flavor and is used in desserts. Red bean paste, made from red adzuki beans, not soybeans, is similar.

PRESERVED VEGETABLE. When you see "Chinese preserved vegetable" listed in a recipe, it usually means preserved mustard greens dusted with chili. You can purchase them in cans or from refrigerated open containers at a Chinese market. Rinse them before cooking, as they can be sandy (the spiciness runs through the vegetable, so don't worry about rinsing off the flavor). Refrigerated in an airtight container, they keep indefinitely.

STRAW MUSHROOMS. These little mushrooms are only available canned and do not have much flavor, but they have a nice silky texture. Drain and rinse them well with cold water before using.

Preserved, Processed, and Dried Ingredients

AGAR-AGAR. Asian cooks use agar-agar, a clear substance extracted from seaweed, in the same way that Western cooks use gelatin. It is the thickening agent in almond "bean curd," the popular Chinese dessert. Like gelatin, agar-agar must be carefully dissolved in liquid to do its work, although unlike gelatin, it does not need to be chilled to set. Also called *kanten,* it often comes in strips that look like crinkled transparent tape, but the flaked version is easiest to measure and use. Look for it in health food stores.

BAMBOO SHOOTS, DRIED. Slender dried bamboo shoots are sold packaged in plastic bags. They must be soaked in hot water until softened, and then drained before using.

BEAN CURD (OR TOFU). The soybean product, made of coagulated soy milk, comes in silken, soft, medium, and firm consistencies and is sold, packaged in plastic containers, in markets everywhere. Choose the consistency called for in the recipe.

BLACK MUSHROOMS, CHINESE DRIED. The price range for these dried shiitake mushrooms is quite wide—the bigger, plumper ones with cracked tops have the meatiest flavor and the firmest texture, and command the highest price. To reconstitute dried mushrooms, soak them in very hot water to cover until softened, about 30 minutes. To speed the process, place the mushrooms and water in a microwave-safe bowl, and microwave on high power for 30 seconds; then let them stand for 10 minutes. Drain, squeeze the excess water from the mushrooms, trim and discard the woody stems, and slice the caps as needed. If you wish, reserve the soaking water to use as a vegetarian soup stock.

CHESTNUTS. Roasting and peeling fresh chestnuts is quite a chore. Fortunately cooked and peeled chestnuts can be found in vacuum-sealed packages at Asian groceries and many supermarkets.

CHILIES, DRIED HOT RED. One of the key ingredients of Sichuan cuisine and red-cooked dishes, these are sold in bags at Asian grocery stores and are quite inexpensive. They are on average 2 inches long and are a deep brick-red color. In some recipes the peppers are fried in oil to subtly flavor the oil.

FERMENTED RICE. This is a moist rice that has been fermented in wine. I've made it optional in the recipes that call for it (except in Baby Ribs Wuxi-Style, where red fermented rice gives the glaze its distinctive color), as it is found only at well-stocked Asian groceries.

LILY BUDS, DRIED. Sometimes called *golden needles,* these dried yellow and orange daylily flowers (not actually buds) must be soaked in hot water and then trimmed of their hard stem parts before using. They have an earthy, slightly sour flavor and a firm yet tender texture, and are indispensable in Hot and Sour Soup.

SESAME PASTE. This is the base for the famous Sichuan sesame sauce that is used with noodles. If you need a substitute, use peanut butter; do not use tahini, the Mediterranean sesame paste.

TREE EARS. Also known as *black fungus* and *cloud ears*. At first impression, the curly, black dried fungi seem small, but when reconstituted in hot water, they expand to three to five times their size, so use them judiciously. While they have very little flavor, their crunchy texture is invaluable in Hot and Sour Soup and other dishes. If you get the larger variety, trim the base area after soaking, as it can be hard. You can occasionally find fresh ones in specialty markets; just estimate the conversion, as you rarely need more than a large handful to provide the right amount of crunchy texture.

WATER CHESTNUT FLOUR. Made of ground dried water chestnuts, this flour makes an especially crispy coating for fried foods, such as Lemon Chicken.

Salted and Cured Meats

CHINESE SAUSAGE. You'll see dried, slightly sweet pork sausages hanging in the meat department in Asian groceries. Before using them, they should be steamed for 10 to 15 minutes, until heated through. (In steamed dishes, they are simply added to the pot or steamer.)

DUCK EGGS, SALTY. These duck eggs have been soaked in brine. Usually just the mildly flavored yolk is used—the whites are too salty.

SMITHFIELD HAM. Smithfield ham is similar to the very firm, salty Yunnan ham, which is a good thing because the Chinese one is not exported. Purchase thick slices of Smithfield ham at a supermarket or deli. Just chop the amount you need, then tightly wrap and refrigerate the leftover ham; it will keep for weeks. To remove some of its saltiness, soak the ham in water to cover for 30 minutes or so before using it.

Condiments and Sauces

BARBECUE SAUCE. This bears no resemblance to a Western barbecue sauce, with its sweet-and-sour tomato base. It is made from ground dried fish, chili peppers, garlic, coriander seeds, and other spices. I like Bull Head brand.

CHINESE BLACK VINEGAR. An aged black vinegar, usually made from grains like rice, wheat, and millet, this is similar to Italian balsamic vinegar, which can be used as a substitute. Look for Kong Yen and Chinkiang brands, which have the fullest flavor.

FERMENTED BEAN CURD. This deeply flavored, salty, slightly cheeselike bean curd comes in two colors: white and red. The red variety, which has been colored with red rice, supplies flavor and bright red color to meat dishes such as barbecued spareribs and braised lamb. Koon Chun is a good brand.

FERMENTED BLACK BEANS. One of the classic flavors of Cantonese cooking, these salty, winey soybeans have turned black from fermentation. They should be rinsed before using, and coarsely chopped and mashed to release their flavor. Stored in an airtight container in a cool, dark cupboard, they keep indefinitely.

FISH SAUCE. This important seasoning of Southeast Asian cuisine also makes an appearance in the dishes at Shun Lee. The clear, amber-colored, and intensely salty liquid is made from brined, fermented anchovies. Buy a Vietnamese or Thai brand; the Filipino fish sauce, called *pastis*, is quite weak. I recommend Lucky and Squid brands. The latter is actually made from squid rather than anchovies, and has a distinct seafood flavor.

GROUND BEAN SAUCE. An ancient ingredient, this thick soybean sauce comes in cans or jars. Black bean sauce is another product altogether. Koon Chun makes a good version.

HOISIN SAUCE. This bean sauce is very sweet, with a slightly spicy, garlicky flavor. It packs a lot of flavor and should be used sparingly. Koon Chun is my preferred brand.

HOT BEAN SAUCE. Sometimes called *ground bean hot sauce,* this is bean sauce flavored with chili peppers. Har Har is a very good brand.

HOT CHILI BEAN SAUCE WITH GARLIC. It is just what it says—bean sauce with plenty of extra spice from chilis and garlic. I recommend Hai Pao Wang.

HOT CHILI (PEPPER) OIL. This fiery red soybean oil is flavored with chili peppers. It is used as a flavoring, not as a cooking oil.

HOT CHILI PASTE. This incendiary paste is made from ground salted, fermented chilies and is sometimes enhanced with garlic and soybeans. It is different from hot chili bean sauce with garlic.

OYSTER SAUCE. This medium-thick brown sauce is made from oysters, water, salt, cornstarch, and caramel. Lee Kum Kee brand has a well-rounded flavor.

RICE WINE. This amber-colored spirit is used in many dishes, so it is worth the effort to search out a good brand from the city of Shaoxing at a liquor store in your nearest Chinese community. Pass up the Chinese rice wine labeled "for cooking" at an Asian grocery, because it is an inferior wine that has been seasoned with salt and/or sugar. Rice wine has a flavor similar to dry sherry, which is a fine substitute; sake, the Japanese rice liquor, is not. Store the wine in a cool dark place at room temperature for up to 3 months. I like the Yuan Hong brand, labeled "Shao Hsing" (the generic Chinese phrase for "rice wine").

SESAME OIL, ASIAN DARK. The beautifully scented amber-colored oil is extracted from toasted sesame seeds. Don't use clear, domestic sesame oil, which is expelled from untoasted seeds and lacks character. The dark sesame oil will burn and lose its fragrance over high heat, so use it as a seasoning oil, and add it to food just before serving. Kadoya and Maruhon are especially good brands.

SOY SAUCE. Go to the soy sauce section of a Chinese market and you will find bottle after bottle of this essential sauce, each variety differing in flavor, intensity, and body. The most common are dark, light, double black, reduced-sodium, and mushroom. The darker the soy sauce, the longer it has been aged, and the more likely it is to be mixed with bead molasses for heavier body and a hint of sweetness. I use regular dark soy sauce for most of the recipes in this book. Beware of bargains, as inexpensive imported brands are often oversalted. Once you find a brand you like, remember it and make it a pantry staple. For general cooking, I prefer Old Label Dark Soy Sauce, but Kikkoman is an acceptable substitute. Koon Chun Double Black Soy Sauce, which has a lovely, rich flavor without being overly salty, is used in the Salmon Fillet with Scallions.

Spices, Flavorings, and Colorings

CINNAMON. At Chinese groceries, you will find bags of cinnamon sticks, which are actually pieces of bark from the cassia tree. It is used to season braised dishes, especially red-cooked ones. Ground cinnamon is one of the ingredients in five-spice powder.

FIVE-SPICE POWDER. A blend of warm, aromatic spices, it is used sparingly in savory dishes. The classic blend includes star anise, cinnamon, cloves, Sichuan peppercorns, and licorice root. According to folklore, each spice represents a different element of the Chinese cosmos. The mix can change a bit from one manufacturer to another.

RED RICE. A specialty of Shanghai, this uncooked rice is naturally dyed red. It is used as a food coloring, not as a side dish.

ROCK SUGAR. These large, hardened amber crystals, made from a mixture of unrefined sugar and honey, are used in braised or red-cooked dishes. Place the crystals in a plastic bag, or wrap them in a piece of cloth, and then coarsely crush them with a meat mallet or a cleaver. If you can't find it, substitute a mixture of equal amounts of white and brown sugar.

RUEY FAH STEAM POWDER. This mix of ground rice with spices (cinnamon, cumin, star anise, and pepper), found in small, inexpensive packets, is used to coat steamed meats. McCormick makes a version labeled "Fen Zheng Rou Seasoning."

SICHUAN PEPPERCORNS. Rust-red Sichuan peppercorns are not really peppercorns, but the berries of another shrub. They have a mentholated spiciness that is totally unique—use too much and it will temporarily numb your mouth. Sichuan peppercorns were banned from the United States for a few years when it was suspected that they might carry a plant disease, but the ban has happily been lifted.

STAR ANISE. A star-shaped pod with six to eight points, each enclosing a dark brown seed, star anise is added whole to infuse braised dishes. Ground, it is an ingredient in five-spice powder. Although it has a licorice-like flavor, it is unrelated to both licorice and anise; it is actually the dried flower head of a Chinese magnolia tree.

THAI KITCHEN TOM YUM HOT AND SOUR SOUP BASE. Thai soups have a lot of ingredients, and I find it easier to use this high-quality product rather than measure out small amounts of spices. The soup base includes Thai chilies, lemongrass, onion, tamarind, sugar, dried shrimp, and other ingredients. It is used in the Hot and Sour Bouillabaisse.

Noodles and Wrappers

BEAN CURD SHEETS. Sold fresh or frozen, these very large (about 30 inches in diameter), round beige sheets are also called *bean curd skins*. They are made by heating soy milk until a skin forms; the skin is lifted off and dried on mats. They serve as a skinlike wrapping for a variety of savory fillings, especially Vegetable "Duck" Pie.

BEAN THREADS, DRIED. Used in the Beijing Lamb Stew recipe, these "thread" noodles are actually quite wide—they look like stiff, wrinkled ribbons of gold-yellow parchment. Don't confuse them with very thin mung bean threads. Sometimes the label will include an illustration of yellow soybeans, which tells you that you have the right item. They need to be soaked in hot water before using.

CHINESE NOODLES. You'll find wheat-flour noodles, both dried and fresh, in Asian markets. Linguine is a good substitute for the dried variety. In either case, the noodles must be boiled before use. The fresh noodles will take just a few minutes; for dried, follow the suggested cooking time on the package.

DRIED RICE FLOUR NOODLES. Also called *rice vermicelli* or *rice sticks,* these hard, white noodles, which come in a range of thicknesses from very thin to wide, must be soaked in warm water before using. Do not boil them. Deep-fried unsoaked noodles will puff up like a white bird's nest and are used for a crunchy garnish.

DUMPLING WRAPPERS. These round, ready-made wrappers are sometimes called *gyoza wrappers* and are sold frozen or in the produce department of Asian and Western markets. If you are near a Chinese community, you will find fresh wrappers, which are slightly larger and more pliable than the supermarket variety. If you don't use an entire package, the leftovers can be tightly wrapped in plastic wrap and refrigerated for up to 1 week. Chop them up and add them to soups, if you aren't making more dumplings. Twin Marquis is a good brand.

MUNG BEAN FLOUR NOODLES. Made from the starch of the mung bean, these thin, clear dried noodles must be soaked in hot water before using. After draining them, you may prefer to snip them into more manageable portions with kitchen scissors. They are also called *cellophane noodles, bean vermicelli, long rice, sai fun,* and *bean threads*. They come in packed in bundles, usually with eight 2-ounce portions to a bag.

PANCAKES. Sometimes labeled *Peking* or *Mandarin pancakes,* you'll want these for when you make Mu Shu Pork. They are available in two sizes, either 4 or 8 inches in diameter, and resemble flour tortillas, which are thicker and should be used as a substitute only in a pinch. Look for them in the frozen food section at an Asian market.

SPRING ROLL WRAPPERS. Used to wrap fillings for deep-fried spring rolls, these paper-thin wrappers fry into a shatteringly crisp texture. Do not confuse them with the thicker and much inferior egg roll wrappers. Wei Chuan makes good spring roll wrappers.

WONTON SKINS. These square wrappers, made of wheat flour, make quick work of preparing homemade wontons. Asian grocers are likely to carry fresh ones; look for the frozen variety if you don't see them in the produce department of your supermarket. The unstuffed wrappers can be frozen; or you can freeze stuffed wontons. Leftover wrappers can be stored just like dumpling wrappers.

Equipment

WHEN DISCUSSING CHINESE COOKING UTENSILS, the dialogue must begin with the wok. Its half-dome shape gives it many uses as a skillet for stir-fries as well as a pot for braises and deep-frying. The wok has a larger cooking surface than a skillet and holds heat beautifully. The bottom of a wok can be flat or round. A 14-inch-diameter, flat-bottomed wok is by far the best choice for most home cooks, as it will sit directly on a gas or electric burner and the size will accommodate a good quantity of food. Round-bottomed woks, while traditional, require a collar or ring over the burner to hold the wok, and this makes for dangerously shaky cooking on most stoves. When you purchase your wok, don't forget to get a lid, which is often sold separately.

While there are easy-to-care-for stainless-steel and nonstick woks, the classic model is made of spun steel or cast iron. While this kind of wok conducts heat extremely well, it requires seasoning before its initial use and special care in washing and drying. To season a new spun-steel or cast-iron wok, wash it well with an abrasive cleaner in hot soapy water to remove the factory residue. This is the last time any soap or cleanser will touch the wok! Dry the wok with a towel, and heat it on the stove over medium heat to dry it thoroughly. Turn off the heat, add 2 tablespoons of flavorless cooking oil, and rub the oil over the entire interior of the wok with paper towels. Heat the wok over low heat for 10 to 15 minutes to allow the metal to soak up the oil. Then wipe out the wok with clean paper towels, which will become dirty from picking up more factory residue. Repeat the oiling, heating, and wiping procedure a couple more times, until the paper towels come away clean. The wok is now ready to use.

When cleaning this kind of wok after each use, never wash it with soap and water, which will remove the cooking oils. You want these oils to build up to form a natural nonstick surface. To clean it, wipe out the food clinging to the interior of the wok, using a wire scrubber, and rinse the wok well with hot water. Then heat the wok over high heat for a minute or so to sterilize it and to ensure that it is thoroughly dry. Let it cool and store it. It is important to dry the wok thoroughly to avoid rusting. If the wok does rust, or if it develops a sticky coating, repeat the "oil, heat, and wipe" seasoning process. Remember, the more you use a wok, the more seasoned it will become, and the less likely it will rust. Get in the habit of using it for Western-style cooking, too, for dishes such as scrambled eggs or a side dish of stir-fried vegetables.

There are two other types of woks available to Western cooks who may find the care of a classic wok daunting (even though it is quite easy). Pricey polished stain-less-steel woks with flat bottoms are sold at kitchenware shops. They are shiny and beautiful but lack the character of a traditional wok, and they are heavy too. You will also find flat-bottomed woks with nonstick interiors, but most cooks feel that the coating inhibits browning during stir-frying. Remember that scores of millions of people cook in plain spun-steel or cast-iron woks every day, and that the old way may be the best.

Some cookbooks suggest substituting a large skillet for a wok. This can be done with recipes that don't require the meat to be "passed through" oil before the final cooking (see page 16). But recipes with the passing-through step need a pool of oil, which can be obtained with the least amount of oil in a deep wok; the wide, flat surface of a skillet requires a wasteful amount of oil. If absolutely necessary, heat the passing-through oil in a medium-size saucepan, then stir-fry the dish in a large skillet.

No matter what kind of wok you use, the key to wok cooking is high heat. The wok should be thoroughly heated over a high flame before you add oil for deep-frying or stir-frying. This helps the oil heat up more quickly and keeps food from sticking to the wok. And keep the heat on high when cooking, so each morsel will cook quickly and retain its texture and individual flavor.

A FEW UTENSILS WILL HELP YOU use your wok with ease. A *wide wire-mesh strainer,* or *skimmer,* lifts the ingredients from the oil after the passing-through step, effectively draining them. You will find it wherever woks are sold. While you can use a *wooden spoon* to stir ingredients as they cook, a special wedge-shaped *metal scoop* is preferable, and will help transfer the food to a platter for serving. *Spring-loaded tongs* are useful for plucking food from oil or broth. You will also need a

Serving Sizes

In most Chinese meals, there are as many main courses as there are diners, but the portions are small.

In this book, most recipes make four small servings for four people, assuming you are cooking four dishes. If, however, you are serving one or two dishes for four people, you should double the recipes. So, in many of the recipes here, we suggest that each dish makes two to four servings, depending on how many other dishes are served.

fine-mesh strainer to remove bits of deep-fried food from the oil when you need to reuse the oil for another step in a recipe. A *deep-frying thermometer* is indispensable for gauging the temperature of oil for passing through and deep-frying. Because of the round sides of a wok, the traditional clip-on thermometers won't work well. Look for digital thermometers with curved probes that can be balanced on the edge of the wok.

The *cleaver* is the primary cutting tool in a Chinese kitchen. Just as the skill of a French chef is measured by how he or she handles a knife, professional Chinese chefs are judged by their work with a cleaver. The chefs at Shun Lee can julienne scallions into gossamer strips without even looking at the chopping board. They possess the artistry of the cleaver that the Chinese have treasured since the Tang Dynasty (A.D. 618–907)

A Chinese cleaver is used to bone fish, slice meat, and chop vegetables. Knives are just as comfortable for some cooks for these jobs. The chefs at Shun Lee peel ginger with a cleaver, but that is an acquired talent—and a marvel to watch. Feel free to peel your ginger with a vegetable peeler.

For steaming, look for a *bamboo or aluminum steamer* that is large enough to hold a bowl or a plate that will contain the finished dish, like a steamed whole bass or a pound of steamed ribs. The steamer sits in a wok or pot to do its job. Finally, you will want (but probably already have) a broiling rack that can be placed on a metal tray that can be filled with a half inch or so of water, which is used for roasting Barbecued Spareribs.

Cooking Chinese Food at Home

WHEN I ORDER A MENU FOR A CUSTOMER, I choose an array of dishes, each cooked in a different way. I will suggest something stir-fried and crunchy, and something else, a fish perhaps, that is poached and silken. Throughout the meal, there will be a harmony of the five flavors: sweet, salty, hot, sour, and a hint, perhaps, of bitter. In home cooking, especially at multi-course dinner parties, I cook a meal the way my mother did: Rather than tying up the stove with dishes that all required wok cooking, she served a steamed or braised dish alongside. This makes sense—it helps to keep the cook sane as well as providing variety to the meal.

No matter how many dishes you make for a meal—whether it's just one dish with some rice and a steamed green vegetable for a weeknight supper or an extravagant banquet for special friends—organizing is essential. Chinese food has a multi-layered depth of flavor, and most recipes include a fairly long list of ingredients. It is imperative that all of the ingredients are measured and prepared before you start cooking. You will find that the bulk of your time will be spent in preparation and not in the actual cooking, which usually goes rather quickly.

A collection of small dishes or ramekins is very helpful for holding the prepared ingredients. Slightly larger bowls can be used to contain the mixed components for a sauce. When the recipe says that the ingredients will be cooked together (such as the ginger, garlic, and scallions for a stir-fry), put them all in one bowl after preparing them. When you are making more than one dish, place the measured and prepared ingredients on separate trays (baking sheets work equally well) for each dish. Read through the recipe to be sure that you understand the timing or any unfamiliar techniques.

When a recipe calls for any kind of nut, like sesame oil, cashews, peanuts, or pine nuts, feel free to eliminate that ingredient if anyone you are cooking for has an allergy to nuts. The absence of nuts won't change the flavor of the dish that much.

Our Sichuanese and Hunanese recipes are spicy, but not overly so. If you want to increase the spiciness, feel free to do so.

"Passing Through"

A key technique in Shanghai and Sichuan cooking is "passing through," where the meat is cooked by passing it through hot oil. This step makes chicken breast meat silken, transforms shrimp into toothsome creatures with a firm, almost crunchy texture, and renders paper-thin strips of pork and steak tender and juicy within. In passing through, the food is very briefly cooked in a pool of hot vegetable oil and then removed from the wok. To finish the dish, almost all of the oil is poured off from the wok, and the remaining oil is used to create the sauce. Finally, the passed-through food is returned to the wok and stir-fried with the sauce.

While passing through is primarily a restaurant technique, it is worthwhile taking the time to master it because no other cooking technique can give the same results. Yes, the food is deep-fried, but if it is done properly, it is not unhealthy. First, the food is always coated with a thin batter of egg white and starch, which helps keep the oil from seeping into the food. We use an unsaturated vegetable oil, such as soybean or canola, which is much better for you than saturated animal fats like lard. And remember that even if you cook with a quart of oil, only a tiny amount will be absorbed by the food. You may consider discarding the cooking oil an extravagance, but it is unwise to save the oil for another use, as it will develop off flavors.

To prepare for the passing-through step in a recipe, place a metal colander on a plate near the stove to hold and drain the fried food. Use a deep-frying thermometer to test the temperature of the oil. Be sure to have a wide wire-mesh strainer for removing the food, and if there is to be a subsequent frying step (as in Crispy Orange Beef), have a fine-mesh strainer handy to skim off any bits of fried batter. Use a large metal wok scoop or spoon to stir the food, as the mesh on the wide strainer could disturb the coating on the meat. Place a large metal can or bowl nearby, for discarding the oil (set it on a heatproof plate if your countertop isn't heat-resistant).

Heat the wok for a few minutes over high heat until it is very hot. If you flick water from your fingertips into the wok, the water should sizzle away on contact. Pour in enough vegetable oil to reach at least 1 inch up the sides of the wok—this will be about 4 cups in a 14-inch flat-bottomed wok. There must be enough oil to completely submerge the food in it. Don't skimp—any food that sticks out of the hot oil will not cook at the same rate as the rest of the food, and it will get soggy too. In some cases, due to the quantity of food, you may need enough oil to reach $1\frac{1}{2}$ to 2 inches up the sides of the wok.

The temperature of the oil is the key to passing through. The oil should be hot enough to cook the food but not hot enough to brown it: 300° to 325°F. (Higher temperatures are reserved for true deep-frying, where the food will develop a crisp golden brown crust.) With the wok preheated, the oil will take only a few minutes to reach the proper temperature. Do not underestimate the value of a deep-frying thermometer. If you don't have one, you can gauge the temperature of the oil with a $\frac{1}{2}$-inch cube of white bread: it should take at least a minute to brown in the hot oil. But unless you are an experienced cook, use the thermometer.

The protein food (meat, poultry, or seafood) will have been marinated in the egg-white/starch coating. Carefully add the food to the hot oil, one or two pieces at a time, taking care that you don't splash the oil. Add the food quickly, but do not dump everything in at once, and try to keep the pieces as separate as possible so they don't stick together. The food will sink to the bottom of the wok, where the oil around it will bubble, but not furiously. The temperature will drop when the cool food is added, so keep the heat on very high to help the oil return to its original temperature. When all of the food has been added, stir the food gently or quickly, depending on the recipe, with the metal scoop to keep the pieces from clinging to each other. Cook until the pieces of chicken, shrimp, or fish turn white on the surface, about 45 seconds; or until pieces of beef or pork turn a light brown (which could take a bit longer, depending on the size of the pieces). Use the strainer to transfer the food to the colander.

In most cases, you will now (carefully!) pour the hot oil into the metal can or bowl, leaving 2 tablespoons of the oil in the wok. Let the oil stand to cool completely in the can before discarding it. If you have a subsequent frying step, be sure to heat the oil in the wok to the required temperature before continuing.

Stir-Frying

Stir-frying—in fact, all cooking in a wok—developed from cooking over a direct flame. Therefore, the Chinese became used to cooking with very high heat (not to discount the slow-cooking methods of braising and poaching). One advantage to high heat is that it sears in moisture and flavor and helps retain crisp textures. While the high flame on a gas stove is preferable, you can get excellent results from a flat-bottomed wok on an electric stove.

After the food has been passed through, all but a couple of tablespoons of the oil are discarded from the wok. The ingredients for the sauce base should be stirred together in a small bowl; if the sauce includes sugar, stir until the sugar has dissolved. In another small bowl, dissolve the thickening agent (almost always cornstarch) in water: Sprinkle the cornstarch over the water and it will dissolve smoothly. If you put cornstarch in the bowl and add water, it will lump. Before adding the sauce and thickener to the wok, stir them to blend in any ingredients that may have settled in the bottom of the bowl.

With the sauce and thickening liquid ready, and the remaining ingredients prepared, you are ready to do the actual stir-frying. Each step will happen very quickly, requiring only about 20 seconds, so you are only a minute or so away from eating.

Return the wok to high heat and heat the oil until it is shimmering, which is the indication that it can't get any hotter without smoking. (Avoid heating oil until it smokes, as that is an indication that the oil is breaking down and the flavor will be altered.) From here, each recipe varies in how the ingredients are added, but in any case, hold the wok with one hand and use the other to stir the ingredients vigorously with the metal wok scoop. The idea is to keep the food in constant motion, so if you are feeling especially athletic, you can shake the wok with one hand while you stir with the other. Thanks to the round sides of the wok, there are many hot surfaces for the food to come into contact with, and it will cook quickly.

Steaming

American cooks reserve steaming for the occasional vegetable, but in Chinese cuisine, steaming is a much-appreciated cooking technique used for many different dishes from seafood to meat. The gentle, moist heat cooks at a moderate rate, retaining the food's natural color, flavor, and texture. While you can sometimes rig a collapsible aluminum steamer over boiling water in a covered pot to steam a dish, an Asian-style steamer is much more efficient. This indispensable item is stored on the stove of many a Chinese kitchen, never hidden away in a cabinet.

There are two kinds of steamers, aluminum and bamboo. In either case, the steamer consists of round stacked racks. The aluminum steamer usually has two wide racks (about 11 inches in diameter) over a bottom compartment, which holds the boiling water. It is by far the best choice, as some recipes call for containing the food to be steamed in bowl or platter, and these utensils will simply not fit in the shallow, narrow bamboo racks. If you are steaming only one item, use the top rack with its deep lid to hold the food (or the food in its utensil), keeping the bottom rack near the water in place. This positions the food away from the steam and allows it to cook at a more relaxed pace.

Inexpensive bamboo steamers, usually consisting of four racks, must be placed over a pot or wok of water. The sides of bamboo steamers will eventually scorch from direct contact with the hot pot or wok. These tiered bamboo steamers are best for cooking many pieces of dim sum. If you don't need all of the racks to hold the food, use the bottom rack to separate the remaining racks from the hottest area of the steam.

In some recipes the ingredients are combined in a covered bowl before steaming, holding in and intensifying the flavors. A stainless-steel bowl and plastic wrap will sometimes suffice, but Asian markets carry a wide range of heatproof ceramic bowls with lids. They're inexpensive, and seem to supply better flavor than the metal bowls. A bowl 9 inches in diameter and about 3 inches deep is a good average-size choice.

No matter what kind of steamer you use, bring a good amount of water to a boil to provide a full head of steam. Cover the steamer tightly, and check the water level occasionally to be sure that it isn't boiling away—add more boiling water from a kettle if needed.

Deep-frying

Biting into the golden-brown coating of Chengdu Chicken or the crisp shell of a freshly cooked spring roll is a sensory treat that is hard to surpass. Deep-frying and only deep-frying provides that irresistible crunch.

One of the secrets of deep-frying is to use enough oil. The oil should truly be deep enough to surround the food. In a wok, you will need to add enough oil to come at least 2 inches up the sides of the wok. If you prefer to use a deep pot, add enough to come at least one-third up the sides. Don't skimp! On the other hand, keep in mind that there will be some bubbling and displacement when the food is added, so don't overfill the cooking utensil.

Equally important, be sure to use a deep-frying thermometer to test the temperature—usually about 350°F, higher than that for the passing-through technique.

If the temperature is too low, the food will cook, but the coating will not crisp. Just as in stir-frying, heat the empty wok over high heat before adding the oil. The oil will heat up more quickly from contact with the piping-hot metal.

Add the food carefully to the hot oil to avoid splashing. Do not crowd the food, as the food will give off steam as it cooks, and this accumulated moisture will affect the crispness of the coating. Some recipes fry the food in two or three brief periods rather than one long one, a trick that creates an especially crunchy coating.

When the food is golden brown, transfer it it from the oil with the wide-mesh strainer to a colander. The colander (or in some cases, such as a whole fried fish, a wire rack set over a rimmed baking sheet) does a better job of draining than paper towels. When the coating comes into contact with the towels, the steam can't escape, and the collected moisture makes the coating soggy. If the oil is needed for subsequent cooking of other ingredients, skim off the bits of browned batter with a fine-mesh skimmer or slotted spoon.

Other Cooking Methods

While American cooks may associate stir-frying, deep-frying, and steaming almost exclusively with Chinese food, the Chinese use a wide range of cooking techniques, including smoking, blanching, pickling, braising, and roasting. Because the latter techniques are a bit more familiar in American kitchens, I won't detail them quite as thoroughly as the others.

Smoking does require a bit of additional explanation, because in these recipes, it will be accomplished indoors in a wok on the stove and not on an outdoor grill. Instead of wood chips, a moist mixture of rice, tea, and spices smolders in a covered, aluminum foil–lined wok (the foil keeps the smoking materials from staining the wok). As the food cooks at a moderate pace, the aromatic smoke deeply infuses the food with incredible flavor. Have a round rack that will fit the wok to hold the food above the smoking mixture. Some woks have such a rack, or use a round cake rack. Adjust the heat so you see just a wisp of smoke—it should not be billowing. Be sure to have the stove exhaust on full to remove the smoke from the kitchen.

Braising, especially the famous red-cooked food of Shanghai, is one of the easiest and most delicious ways to create a meal, yet the end result is a symphony of deep, complex tastes. In braising, the food is slowly simmered in liquid, making for an exchange of flavors and succulent meat. In red-cooking, which seems to be the most popular cooking technique in Chinese homes, the liquid always includes soy sauce, sugar, and spices, which impart a reddish tinge to the food. Usually this liquid is boiled down at the end of cooking to make an intensely flavored, syrupy sauce. Some cooks refrigerate their braising liquid to use over and over again, but for safe storage reasons, it is a better idea to discard the leftovers. Braising is best accomplished in a heavy flameproof casserole, such as an enameled cast-iron Dutch oven, but any sturdy pot with a tight-fitting lid will do. Keep the flame low so the food cooks at a steady simmer, and keep an eye on the pot, as the sugar in the sauce loves to caramelize (which is a short step away from burning).

When a Chinese cook talks about pickling, it isn't always the technique of storing food for a long time in salt or vinegar. And this pickling will not involve glass jars immersed in a hot water bath. Pickled vegetables in the Chinese fashion are often more marinated than pickled. The salt and vinegar are used for their texture-changing and seasoning properties, and long preservation is not always the goal. The Chinese may not be fond of raw vegetable salads, but they love pickled vegetables.

In many of these recipes, we recommend blanching vegetables in homemade or canned chicken broth, then discarding the broth. Blanching both partially cooks the vegetables, while heightening their color. The Shun Lee chefs prefer blanching in broth to plain water because the former adds flavor to the process. However, if you find discarding the broth wasteful, consider storing the broth to use as a soup base. You can also substitute water, or a mixture of water and broth, for the broth alone.

Roasting is not used much in Chinese homes because the vast majority of kitchens do not have ovens. Roasted dishes, such as Beijing duck, are reserved for very special occasions and prepared by chefs at oven-equipped banquet halls. In fact, there are precious few roasted dishes in this book.

Hot Appetizers

AS FIRST COURSES before the main meal, traditional Chinese appetizers are usually cold dishes, like Drunken Chicken. As enticing and appetite-arousing as they may be, small hot dishes like spring rolls and dumplings are considered snacks, and are eaten between meals. In China, dumplings and steamed buns stuffed with pork and vegetables are sold throughout the day as street food. Alone, dumplings are considered an entire meal when eaten at home. However, at Shun Lee we serve these hot nibbles in the Western fashion, as appetizers.

Some of these "small plate" dishes belong to the dim sum family. These charming bite-sized morsels (dim sum means "to touch the heart") originated in Canton as foods to go with breakfast and lunchtime tea, although they are now consumed all over the world, in either authentic or fusion form. Hong Kong has become the city best known for its dim sum, and dim sum emporiums there are open from the crack of dawn to late afternoon to handle the demand before and after lunch.

IN CANTON AND HONG KONG, chefs traditionally barbecued duck, goose, and pork, but it wasn't until Cantonese chefs opened restaurants in the United States in the early 1920s that they began to barbecue spareribs to appeal to their American customers. "Barbecued" may not be the proper term, as that means slow-cooked, smoke-infused meat, and these ribs are roasted in an oven. By roasting the ribs on a rack over water, the steam prevents the fat dripping off the ribs from smoking.   **Makes 4 servings**

Barbecued Spareribs

One 2 1/2-pound rack spareribs
Scant 3/4 cup ketchup
1/3 cup sugar
Two 1-inch cubes red fermented bean curd, drained and mashed, optional
2 tablespoons rice wine or dry sherry
2 tablespoons ground bean sauce
1 large egg, lightly beaten
1 tablespoon peeled and minced garlic
2 teaspoons baking soda
1 teaspoon salt
1/2 teaspoon five-spice powder
2 tablespoons honey

1. Lightly score the meaty part of the ribs in a 1-inch diamond pattern. Turn the rack over and nick the membrane at the edge of the rack. Holding the membrane with a kitchen towel, pull it off the bones. Place the ribs in a dish or pan large enough to hold them in a flat layer, and set it aside.

2. Whisk the ketchup, sugar, red fermented bean curd if using, rice wine, bean sauce, egg, garlic, baking soda, salt, five-spice powder, and 1 tablespoon of the honey in a medium bowl until smooth (the baking soda, which is used as a tenderizer, will make the sauce foam). Pour the sauce over the ribs. Using a rubber spatula, rub the sauce into both sides of the ribs. Let stand at room temperature for 1 hour, turning the ribs after 30 minutes.

3. Position a rack in the center of the oven and preheat to 450°F. Place a broiler rack inside a broiler pan or large roasting pan. Oil the broiler rack and fill the pan with ½ inch of water. Arrange the ribs on the rack, meaty side up, reserving the sauce left in the dish. Roast until the top begins to darken to medium red-brown, 20 to 25 minutes. Turn the ribs over and spread with ½ cup of the reserved sauce (discard the remaining sauce). Reduce the temperature to 375°F, and continue cooking until the bony side of the ribs begins to darken to medium red-brown, about 20 minutes. Increase the heat to 500°F. Turn the ribs again so that the meaty side is up. Roast until the sauce is darkened but not burned and the meat is tender, about 20 minutes. (The ribs can be cooked 1 day in advance, cooled, wrapped in aluminum foil, and refrigerated. Reheat the unwrapped ribs in a preheated 400°F oven until heated through, about 15 minutes.)

4. Transfer the ribs to a cutting board, and brush both sides with the remaining 1 tablespoon honey. Slice the ribs into individual pieces, and serve.

Tea

The Chinese love tea, and they drink different teas before, during, and after a meal. They make much of the distinction between green and black teas. In China, the latter is actually called a red tea, because of the final color of the steeped beverage.

Light-bodied green teas, like jasmine, are consumed before a meal, where the subtleties in taste and fragrance can be appreciated. During a meal, Pu Erh or Po Nee is served: black (red) teas with stronger flavors that can stand up to food and help you digest. After dinner, the mild, sweet taste of oolong is soothing. Strongly flavored teas, like Lapsang Souchong or a sweetened chrysanthemum tea, are best savored separately, and not with food.

IN BOTH MANDARIN AND CANTONESE, the word *soong* means "minced." This delicate dish of minced chicken and finely diced vegetables served in lettuce cups is an adaptation of a Cantonese banquet dish of minced squab served in lettuce. It makes a fine light lunch dish, too.   **Makes 4 servings**

Chicken Soong in Lettuce Wrap

Chicken
8 ounces boneless, skinless chicken breast, cut into $1/4$-inch cubes
$1^1/2$ teaspoons egg white (beat the white until foamy, then measure)
1 teaspoon cornstarch
$1/8$ teaspoon salt
Vegetable oil, for passing through

Sauce
2 tablespoons soy sauce
1 tablespoon red wine vinegar
1 tablespoon rice wine or dry sherry
$1/2$ tablespoon sugar
1 teaspoon ground white pepper
1 teaspoon cornstarch

4 celery ribs, strings removed with a vegetable peeler, finely diced (1 cup)
4 scallions, white and green parts, trimmed and minced ($3/4$ cup)
3 carrots, finely diced ($1/2$ cup)
1 teaspoon dark sesame oil
2 teaspoons hoisin sauce
8 whole Bibb or iceberg lettuce leaves
2 tablespoons lightly toasted pine nuts (see Note)

1. To prepare the chicken, place the diced chicken in a medium bowl. Add the egg white, cornstarch, and salt; toss to coat.

2. To prepare the sauce, whisk the soy sauce, vinegar, rice wine, sugar, and white pepper in a small bowl. Dissolve the cornstarch in 1 tablespoon water in another small bowl. Set the bowls aside.

3. Heat a large wok over high heat. Add enough oil to come 1 inch up the sides of the wok and heat it to 300°F. Add the chicken and stir gently, keeping the pieces

from sticking together, until they turn white, about 45 seconds. Using a wide wire-mesh skimmer, transfer the chicken to a colander to drain. Discard all the oil except for 2 tablespoons.

4. Heat the wok with the oil over high heat. Add the celery, scallions, and carrots, and stir-fry until crisp-tender, about 45 seconds. Return the chicken to the wok. Stir the sauce, add it to the wok, and stir-fry for 20 seconds. Add the cornstarch mixture and stir-fry until the chicken is cooked through and the sauce has thickened, about 30 seconds. Stir in the sesame oil. Transfer the chicken mixture to a serving bowl.

5. To serve, spread about $\frac{1}{4}$ teaspoon hoisin sauce in the center of each lettuce leaf. Add 3 tablespoons of the chicken mixture, and sprinkle with a few pine nuts. Place 2 filled lettuce leaves on each plate and serve immediately.

Note: To toast pine nuts, heat an empty wok or skillet over medium-high heat. Add the pine nuts and cook, stirring often, until golden and lightly toasted. Immediately turn the nuts out onto a plate to cool.

THIS DIM SUM FROM HONG KONG clearly illustrates how layers of textures and flavors make Chinese food extraordinary. Whole large shrimp, a shrimp–bamboo shoot paste, and a battered soybean wrapper, deep-fried until crisp, all come into play here. Use the biggest shrimp you can find—they are sometimes labeled "U-15," which means that there are fewer than 15 to a pound.

Makes 4 servings

Crispy Shrimp Wrapped in Soybean Sheets

8 colossal or jumbo shrimp, about $1\frac{1}{4}$ ounces each, peeled and deveined, with the tail left on
1 tablespoon cornstarch

Shrimp Paste
$\frac{1}{2}$ pound medium shrimp, peeled and deveined
$\frac{1}{2}$ cup canned sliced bamboo shoots, drained and rinsed
1 tablespoon sugar
$1\frac{1}{2}$ teaspoons dark sesame oil
$\frac{3}{4}$ teaspoon salt
$\frac{1}{8}$ teaspoon ground white pepper

Batter
$\frac{1}{4}$ cup all-purpose flour
$\frac{1}{4}$ teaspoon baking soda
$\frac{1}{4}$ teaspoon vegetable oil
Pinch of salt

8 bean curd sheets, cut into pieces 6 inches by 3 inches
Vegetable oil, for deep-frying

1. Place the colossal shrimp in a medium bowl. Add the cornstarch and 1 tablespoon water. Massage the shrimp well with the cornstarch mixture, and let stand for 3 minutes. Then rinse them well under cold running water, and drain. Pat the shrimp with paper towels until dry.

2. To make the shrimp paste, place the medium shrimp on a cutting board and mash them, using the flat side of a cleaver or a large, heavy knife. Pulse the bamboo shoots in a food processor until finely chopped. Add the mashed shrimp to the processor and pulse until minced into a paste. Add the sugar, sesame oil, salt, and white pepper, and pulse to combine. Transfer the paste to a small bowl.

3. To make the batter, whisk the flour, baking soda, vegetable oil, salt, and $1/4$ cup cold water in medium bowl until smooth.

4. Combine the shrimp and 2 teaspoons of the batter in a medium bowl, and toss to coat. Lay 1 bean curd sheet on a work surface with the short end facing you. Place a heaping tablespoon of shrimp paste in the center of the bean curd sheet, and spread it to within 2 inches of the long ends. Place a shrimp at the bottom edge of the paste, letting its tail protrude over one side, and place another tablespoon of the shrimp paste on top of the shrimp, lightly spreading it so that it is of even thickness. Roll the bean curd sheet into a cylinder as though forming a cigar, and seal the edge with a smear of the batter. Place the finished roll on a baking sheet. Repeat with the remaining ingredients. (The wrapped shrimp can be prepared 4 hours in advance, covered tightly in a container, and refrigerated. Store the batter at room temperature, and thin it slightly with water to return it to its original consistency before using.)

5. Heat a large wok over high heat. Add enough oil to come about $1\frac{1}{2}$ inches up the sides of the wok, and heat it to 375°F. Holding each shrimp by its tail, dip the shrimp in the batter, letting the excess batter drip off. Add the shrimp to the oil and deep-fry, turning them occasionally, until they are golden brown (but not dark brown) and cooked through, about 2 to $2\frac{1}{2}$ minutes. Using a wide wire-mesh strainer, transfer the shrimp rolls to paper towels to drain. Serve immediately.

YOU WILL FIND SCALLION PANCAKES in Beijing and Shanghai. We serve a thinner, more delicate version at Shun Lee. These are easy to make, and are best eaten freshly fried and piping hot. **Makes 14 pancakes, or 4 to 6 servings**

Scallion Pancakes

Dough

1 1/4 cups all-purpose flour, plus more as needed
1 tablespoon solid vegetable shortening
1 tablespoon vegetable oil
1/4 teaspoon dark sesame oil
1/4 teaspoon salt

Filling

8 scallions, white and green parts, sliced into 1/4-inch pieces (3 1/2 cups)
1/2 cup solid vegetable shortening
1 teaspoon dark sesame oil
1 teaspoon salt

2 tablespoons vegetable oil, plus more as needed

1. To make the dough, combine the flour, shortening, vegetable oil, sesame oil, salt, and 1/2 cup water in a bowl. Mix until the dough comes together.

2. Lightly dust a work surface with flour. Turn out the dough and knead it, folding it over from bottom to top and adding sprinkles of flour as necessary to keep the dough from sticking, about 25 times, or until the dough is smooth and elastic. Place the dough in a sealed plastic bag to keep it moist while you make the filling.

3. To make the filling, mix the scallions, shortening, sesame oil, and salt in a medium bowl until thoroughly blended.

4. To assemble the pancakes, lightly dust the work surface again with flour. Divide the dough in half, and form the halves into cylinders, each about 1 inch in diameter. Cut each cylinder into seven 1/2-inch-thick rounds. Using a rolling pin, roll each round into a 1/8- to 1/4-inch-thick oval, about 8 inches long and 4 inches wide.

5. Place a heaping tablespoon of the scallion mixture in the center of a pancake, and spread it to within 1 to 2 inches of the edge. Roll the top half of the pancake to the

center, and then fold the top in half again, so that there is a double fold on top. Roll up the bottom half of the pancake to the center to meet the top half. Fold the pancake in half horizontally. You will now have a tube. Gently pull the tubular pancake horizontally, so it stretches 1 to 2 inches. Bring the edges of the tube together in a circle, and tuck one end of the tube into the other end, between the double fold, and pinch it tight so that the pancake won't unfold when it is cooked. With the palm of your hand or the side of a cleaver, flatten the pancake into a 4-inch-diameter round about $3/4$ inch thick. Repeat with the remaining dough and filling. (The uncooked pancakes can be made up to 12 hours in advance. Place them in a single layer in a plastic container, cover, and refrigerate.)

6. Heat the vegetable oil in a large skillet (or use two skillets to speed the procedure) over medium heat. Add a pancake to the skillet and press it gently with a metal spatula until it is $4^1/2$ inches in diameter. Cook the pancake, pressing it occasionally with the spatula, until the underside is crisp and golden, about 3 minutes. Turn the pancake over and fry until the other side is golden, about 3 minutes. Transfer it to paper towels to drain. Repeat with the remaining pancakes, adding more oil as needed. Cut each pancake into wedges and serve immediately.

YOU WON'T FIND ACTUAL HONEY in this recipe—Chinese cooks often use the word to describe glazed food. But the lack of honey doesn't matter, since these walnuts are addictive as a nibble with cocktails. They also show up as a garnish on savory dishes, and you might like them in a Western-style green salad with fruit.

Makes 8 servings

Honey-Glazed Walnuts

1½ teaspoons baking soda
1 pound shelled walnut halves
1½ cups sugar
Vegetable oil, for deep-frying

1. Bring 3 cups of water to a boil in a wok over high heat. Stir in the baking soda, and then add the walnuts. Cook for 5 minutes, stirring occasionally. (The baking soda removes some of the outer coating of the walnuts, so the water will foam and turn brown. This step also softens the walnuts and makes them absorb the syrup better.)

2. Drain the walnuts in a colander, and rinse them well under cold running water. Rinse and drain two more times. Drain the walnuts well. Rinse the wok well and wipe it clean.

3. Bring 2 cups of water to a boil in the clean wok over high heat. Add the sugar and boil, stirring often, until it is dissolved and the mixture is syrupy, about 2 minutes. Add the walnuts and return the syrup to a low boil over medium heat. Cook, stirring the walnuts occasionally to keep them from scorching, until the syrup has reduced to a thick glaze that clings to the walnuts, 11 to 14 minutes. Strain the nuts in a large colander, and drain until quite dry, 5 to 10 minutes.

4. Discard the remaining syrup in the wok, and clean the wok well. Add enough oil to come about 2 inches up the sides of the wok, and heat it over high heat to 350°F. In batches, add the walnuts and cook, stirring occasionally, until mahogany brown, 2 to 3 minutes. Using a wide wire-mesh strainer, transfer the walnuts to a dry colander. Drain well, and then spread them out on a baking sheet to cool completely. Store the walnuts in an airtight container at room temperature for up to 1 week.

Cantonese Honeyed Walnuts: As soon as the walnuts have been transferred to the baking sheet, sprinkle them with 2 teaspoons sesame seeds.

IN NORTHERN CHINA, dumplings have a symbolic meaning, and because they signify prosperity, they are always served at New Year's celebrations. We serve mountains of these dumplings every day at Shun Lee because people love them. The dumplings are steamed and then shallow-fried until their bottoms are golden brown, so they are sometimes called pot-stickers. And now that you can buy dumpling wrappers in supermarkets, making them at home has never been easier.

Makes 20 dumplings, or 4 servings

Pan-Fried Pork Dumplings

Filling
- 8 leaves Napa cabbage, finely chopped
- Pinch of salt
- 6 ounces ground pork
- 2 scallions, white and green parts, minced
- 1 tablespoon soy sauce
- 1 tablespoon Chicken Stock (page 70) or canned chicken broth
- 1 tablespoon vegetable oil
- 2 teaspoons dark sesame oil

- 2 tablespoons cornstarch, plus more for sprinkling
- 20 dumpling wrappers (freeze the remaining wrappers in the package)
- 2 tablespoons vegetable oil

Dipping Sauce
- 1 tablespoon soy sauce
- 1 tablespoon Chinese black or balsamic vinegar
- 1 teaspoon dark sesame oil

1. To prepare the filling, mix the cabbage with the salt in a medium bowl. Let it stand for 10 minutes while the cabbage releases its excess water. Meanwhile, combine the pork, scallions, soy sauce, stock, vegetable oil, and sesame oil in another bowl. Transfer the cabbage to a clean kitchen towel and squeeze it hard to release any excess liquid. Add the cabbage to the pork mixture, and mix well. Cover, and freeze for 1 hour (or refrigerate overnight) to firm the mixture so it becomes easier to handle.

2. Dissolve the cornstarch in 3 tablespoons of cold water in a small bowl to make a paste. Line a baking sheet with waxed paper, and sprinkle it with additional cornstarch. Moisten the edges of one dumpling wrapper by dipping your finger into the paste and running it over the edge of the wrapper. Using a blunt knife as a scoop, place about a tablespoon of the filling in the center of the wrapper. Fold the wrapper in half, and pinch the edges closed. Place it on the baking sheet. Repeat with the remaining filling and wrappers. (The uncooked dumplings can be made ahead, covered with plastic wrap, and refrigerated for up to 1 day. Or freeze them for up to 3 months. To freeze, place them in a single layer, pinched side up, in a plastic storage container or plastic storage bag, arranged so that the dumplings don't touch one another. When you are ready to cook them, the frozen dumplings will be easy to remove, one by one.)

3. To make the dipping sauce, mix the soy sauce, vinegar, and sesame oil in a small bowl. Set it aside.

4. Pour an inch or two of water into the bottom of an Asian-style steamer, and bring it to a boil. Lightly oil a dish or plate to hold the dumplings. Arrange the dumplings side by side in the dish, pinched side up, without touching one another. Place the dish in the steamer and cover it. Steam until the filling in the dumplings feels firm when pressed, about 5 minutes. Using tongs, remove the plate from the steamer.

5. Heat the 2 tablespoons oil in a very large skillet over high heat until it shimmers. Carefully add the dumplings, pinched side up, and cook until the bottoms are golden, about 2 minutes. Serve hot, with a communal bowl of the dipping sauce.

HERE IS ANOTHER DISH that is popular in the Canton–Hong Kong culinary corridor, where chefs are most likely to use live shrimp, complete with heads. Because the shrimp are poached in a lightly seasoned stock, their quality is very important, so even if it is unlikely that you will use live shrimp, search for the best-quality thawed frozen shrimp. It is served with a light, slightly spicy dipping sauce.

Makes 2 to 4 servings

Poached Whole Shrimp with Ginger, Scallion, and Soy

Dipping Sauce

2 tablespoons soy sauce

1 tablespoon Maggi Sauce (see Note)

1 tablespoon Chicken Stock (page 70) or canned chicken broth

1 teaspoon peeled and minced fresh ginger

$\frac{1}{2}$ teaspoon Chinese barbecue sauce, preferably Bull Head

1 tablespoon rice wine or dry sherry

1 scallion, white part only, trimmed and minced

1 tablespoon chopped cilantro

1 small green chili, such as Thai or serrano, seeds and ribs removed, minced

1 scallion, green part only, trimmed and cut into 3 pieces

One $\frac{1}{2}$-inch piece peeled fresh ginger, cut into 2 slices and smashed

1 teaspoon rice wine or dry sherry

12 colossal or jumbo shrimp (about $1\frac{1}{4}$ ounces each), unpeeled

1. To make the dipping sauce, mix the soy sauce, Maggi Sauce, stock, ginger. barbecue sauce, rice wine, scallion, cilantro, and chili in a small bowl. Set it aside.

2. Bring 3 cups of water to a boil in a wok over high heat. Add the scallion, ginger, and rice wine. Add the shrimp and cook just until they turn bright pink, about 2 to 3 minutes. Drain well. Discard the scallion and ginger.

3. Transfer the hot shrimp to a platter and arrange, overlapping, in a circle. Serve with the dipping sauce.

Note: Maggi Sauce is a proprietary brand of seasoning sauce that is widely available at supermarkets.

ALONG WITH EGG FOO YUNG and chow mein, these crispy, golden triangles are a Chinese-American invention that is virtually unknown in China. Shun Lee served Sesame Shrimp Toast throughout the '60s and '70s, and although it is no longer on the menu, if you ask for it, the chefs are happy to make it. You can mince the shrimp and water chestnuts separately in a food processor, but use a knife to mince the scallions—they will give off too much chlorophyll in a processor and tint the shrimp mixture green.   **Makes 5 to 6 shrimp toasts, or 4 to 6 servings**

Sesame Shrimp Toast

8 ounces medium shrimp, peeled and deveined

$1/4$ cup minced water chestnuts

2 scallions, white part only, trimmed and minced

3 large egg whites

1 tablespoon cornstarch

2 teaspoons vegetable oil, plus more for deep-frying

$1/2$ teaspoon salt

$1/2$ teaspoon ground white pepper

5 to 6 slices fine-grained white bread, such as Pepperidge Farm, crusts removed

5 to 6 teaspoons black or white sesame seeds (see Note)

1. Pulse the shrimp in a food processor until very finely minced. In a medium bowl, combine the shrimp, water chestnuts, scallions, 2 of the egg whites, cornstarch, 2 teaspoons vegetable oil, salt, and white pepper. Mix until thoroughly blended. (The shrimp mixture can be made up to 12 hours ahead, covered, and refrigerated.)

2. Place the remaining egg white in a small bowl and beat until foamy. Using a table-spoon, first dip the spoon into the egg white, and then scoop up a spoonful of the shrimp mixture. Spread the shrimp over a slice of bread. (The egg white will help the shrimp mixture adhere to the bread.) Sprinkle with about 1 teaspoon of the sesame seeds. Repeat with the remaining ingredients.

3. Heat a large, heavy saucepan over high heat. Add enough oil to come about 2 inches up the sides, and heat it to 350°F. Working in batches without crowding, add 2 to 3 slices of bread, a slice at a time, shrimp side down, to the oil. Deep-fry until the

underside turns golden and the shrimp mixture turns white, about 1 to 1½ minutes. (The time will vary depending on the thickness of the shrimp paste.) Turn the bread over and fry until the underside is golden, about 30 seconds. Using a slotted spatula or a wide wire-mesh strainer, transfer the toasts to paper towels to drain, shrimp side up. Reheat the oil to 350°F and repeat with the remaining bread. Slice each piece of toast diagonally twice, to make four triangles. Serve immediately.

Note: Sesame seeds are inexpensive at Asian grocery stores. Look for black sesame seeds, which will give the toasts a dramatic look. Or use the familiar white sesame seeds, or a combination of the two.

SPRING ROLLS BEAR NO RESEMBLANCE to the heavy, doughy egg rolls that are familiar to American diners. Hailing from Shanghai, spring rolls are elegant and delicate, and when you bite into them, the crisp skin shatters into golden shards. They are great on their own, or you can serve bowls of plum sauce or chutney and Chinese hot mustard for dipping. One very important tip: Be sure the filling is quite dry, as any moisture will seep into the wrapper and tear it.

Makes 12 rolls, 4 to 6 servings

Shanghai Spring Rolls

Filling

3 ounces boneless, skinless chicken breast, cut into thin
    1-inch-long strips about $1/4$ inch wide
$1/2$ large egg white (beat a whole egg white until foamy and measure out half)
1 tablespoon cornstarch
4 cups Chicken Stock (page 70), canned chicken broth, or water
1 pound fresh bean sprouts
$1/3$ cup thinly sliced canned bamboo shoots (1 inch long)
4 Chinese dried black mushrooms, soaked until soft, trimmed,
    and cut into thin $1 1/2$-inch-long strips
$1/2$ carrot, peeled and cut into thin 1-inch-long strips
1 teaspoon salt
3 ounces medium shrimp, peeled, deveined, and finely chopped
1 bunch (3 ounces) fresh chives, cut into $1 1/2$-inch-long lengths
2 tablespoons dark sesame oil
Pinch of ground white pepper

Vegetable oil, for passing through and deep-frying
1 large egg
12 spring roll wrappers
Chinese plum sauce or mango chutney sauce, optional
Chinese mustard, optional

1. For the filling, mix the chicken, egg white, and cornstarch in a small bowl. Coat the chicken well, and set aside.

2. Bring the stock to a boil in a large wok over high heat. Add the bean sprouts, bamboo shoots, mushrooms, carrot, and salt. Cook over high heat for 2 minutes. Add the shrimp and chives, and cook for 1 minute more. Drain in a colander. Transfer the mixture to a clean cloth kitchen towel, and twist the cloth to squeeze out the excess moisture. Squeeze as hard as you can, as the mixture should be as dry as possible. Transfer the mixture to a medium bowl, and mix in the sesame oil and white pepper. Clean the wok.

3. Heat the wok over high heat. Add enough oil to come 1 inch up the sides of the wok, and heat it to 300°F. Add the chicken and stir gently to keep the pieces from sticking together, until they turn white, about 45 seconds. Using a wide wire-mesh strainer, transfer the chicken to the bamboo shoot mixture. Cover, and place the mixture in the freezer for 10 minutes to make it easier to handle. Discard the oil. (If you want to reuse the oil for deep-frying the spring rolls, carefully strain it through a fine-mesh strainer into a heatproof bowl to remove any bits of coating.) Clean and dry the wok.

4. In a small bowl, beat the egg until frothy. On a cutting board, place a spring roll wrapper with a point facing you. Using a tablespoon, place a heaping spoonful of the chicken and bamboo shoot mixture on the bottom third of the wrapper, and spread it out horizontally so that the filling is $2\frac{1}{2}$ inches wide. Roll the bottom point of the wrapper over the mixture, fold the sides in, brush some beaten egg over the top point of the wrapper, and finish rolling the wrapper from bottom to top. Place the roll on a baking sheet. Repeat with the remaining filling and wrappers. (The shrimp rolls can be made up to 2 hours in advance, covered loosely with plastic wrap, and refrigerated.)

5. Heat the wok over high heat. Add enough oil to come about 2 inches up the sides of the wok, and heat it to 350°F. Working in batches without crowding, deep-fry the spring rolls, turning them once, until golden brown, about 2 to 3 minutes. Using a wide wire-mesh skimmer, transfer them to paper towels to drain. Cut each roll in half diagonally and serve immediately, with bowls of plum sauce and mustard on the side for dipping, if desired.

WHILE SCALLOPS ARE PLENTIFUL IN CHINA, cooks there prefer dried scallops rather than fresh ones. I blended the flavors of Cantonese cooking with the sweet taste of fresh scallops to create this sophisticated dish. You must use fresh scallops of the highest quality for this dish, never thawed frozen ones that have been soaked in preservatives. Look for very large day-boat or diver scallops at the best fishmongers.

Makes 2 to 4 servings

Steamed Scallops with Black Bean Sauce

5 scallions, white and green parts, trimmed: 2 left whole, 3 minced
Four $1/8$-inch-thick slices peeled fresh ginger, plus
    $1/2$ teaspoon peeled and minced fresh ginger
4 fresh day-boat or diver scallops
4 scallop shells for cooking (coquilles St. Jacques shells, available
    at kitchenware shops) or small ramekins
3 tablespoons vegetable oil
3 garlic cloves, peeled and minced
$1^1/2$ teaspoons minced Chinese fermented black beans
1 tablespoon seeded and minced red or
    green fresh hot chilies, such as Thai or serrano
1 tablespoon minced cilantro
$1^1/2$ tablespoons sugar
1 tablespoon rice wine or dry sherry
1 tablespoon soy sauce
$1/4$ cup Chicken Stock (see page 70) or canned chicken broth

1. Bring 4 cups of water to a boil in a wok over high heat. Add the whole scallions, ginger slices, and scallops. Cook just until the edges of the scallops begin to firm, about 1 minute. Drain in a colander. Discard the scallions and ginger. Place 1 scallop in each scallop shell.

2. Bring about 1 inch of water to a boil in the bottom of an Asian-style steamer. Heat 2 tablespoons of the vegetable oil in a wok over high heat. Add the minced scallions, garlic, and black beans, and stir-fry until the scallions are wilted, about 20 seconds.

Add the chilies and cilantro, and stir-fry until the cilantro is wilted, about 20 seconds. Add the minced ginger, sugar, rice wine, soy sauce, and stock, and heat to boiling. Spoon the sauce over the scallops. Place the scallop shells on a plate, set it in the steamer, cover, and steam just until the scallops turn white, about 1 to 1½ minutes.

3. Heat the remaining 1 tablespoon vegetable oil in a small skillet over high heat until shimmering. Pour it over the scallops, and serve immediately.

FRIED DUMPLINGS HAVE LEGIONS OF FANS, but there is something soul-fully satisfying about the simplicity of their boiled cousins. What gives character to these boiled dumplings is the wonderful dipping sauce, seasoned with spicy sesame oil.

Makes 20 dumplings, or 4 servings

Sichuan Boiled Dumplings with Spicy Dipping Sauce

Filling

8 ounces ground pork

2 ounces small shrimp, peeled, deveined, and minced

1 tablespoon soy sauce

1 tablespoon vegetable oil

1 tablespoon minced cilantro

1 scallion, green and white parts, trimmed and minced

1 Chinese dried black mushroom, soaked until softened, stem trimmed, and cap minced

1 teaspoon dark sesame oil

$\frac{1}{4}$ teaspoon ground white pepper

2 tablespoons cornstarch, plus more for sprinkling

About 20 round dumpling wrappers

Sauce

2 tablespoons vegetable oil

2 scallions, white part only, trimmed and minced

5 garlic cloves, peeled and minced

1 tablespoon freshly ground black pepper

2 tablespoons sugar

2 tablespoons Chinese black or balsamic vinegar

2 tablespoons hot bean paste

1 tablespoon soy sauce

1 tablespoon dark sesame oil

1 tablespoon hot chili oil

1. For the filling, combine the pork, shrimp, soy sauce, vegetable oil, cilantro, scallion, mushroom, sesame oil, white pepper, and $\frac{1}{3}$ cup water in a medium bowl. Mix well.

Cover, and freeze for 1 hour (or refrigerate overnight) to firm the mixture and make it easier to handle.

2. Dissolve the cornstarch in 3 tablespoons cold water in a small bowl to make a paste. Line a baking sheet with waxed paper and sprinkle it with cornstarch. Moisten the edges of a dumpling wrapper by dipping your finger into the paste and running it over the edge of the wrapper. Using a blunt knife as a scoop, place about a tablespoon of the filling in the center of the wrapper. Bring the edges of the wrapper up to meet at the top of the filling and pinch them closed, squeezing the dough. Place the dumpling on the baking sheet. Repeat with the remaining filling and wrappers. (The uncooked dumplings can be made ahead, covered with plastic wrap, and refrigerated for up to 1 day. Or freeze them for up to 3 months. To freeze, place them in a single layer in a plastic storage container or plastic storage bag, arranged so that the dumplings don't touch one another. When you are ready to cook them, the frozen dumplings will be easy to remove, one by one.)

3. Bring a large saucepan of water to a boil over high heat. Add the dumplings and cover the pan. Cook until the filling is cooked through and the dumplings are floating on top of the water, about 4 minutes.

4. While the dumplings are cooking, make the sauce: Heat a wok or medium skillet over high heat. Add the oil and heat until it shimmers. Add the scallions, garlic, and black pepper, and stir-fry for 20 seconds. Transfer to a small bowl. Add the sugar, vinegar, hot bean paste, soy sauce, sesame oil, and hot chili oil to the scallions, and mix well. Divide the sauce among four soup bowls.

5. Carefully drain the dumplings in a colander. Place the dumplings on top of the sauce in the bowls, and serve immediately.

SHAOXING IS FAMOUS FOR ITS RICE WINE—and for Drunken Chicken, where juicy poached chicken is soaked in a luscious, if heady, wine sauce. The chicken should marinate at least 8 hours or as long as overnight, but not more because the wine will become bitter. You can add a tablespoon or two more of Shaoxing wine when you serve the chicken, for an added dose of flavor. If you can't find a whole chicken breast, use two chicken breast halves with skin and bone, and cook them for only 12 minutes. **Makes 2 to 4 servings**

Drunken Chicken

1 whole chicken breast with skin and bone (about 1 pound)

Sauce

1 scallion, white part only

One 4-inch-long piece fresh ginger, peeled and cut into 6 pieces

$3/4$ cup Chicken Stock (page 70) or canned chicken broth

$1/4$ cup rice wine or dry sherry

1 teaspoon salt

$1/4$ teaspoon sugar

6 cilantro sprigs, for garnish

1. Bring 8 cups of water to a near boil in a medium saucepan over high heat. Add the chicken and cook for 2 minutes. Cover the pot, turn off the heat, and poach the chicken until the meat has turned white and is just cooked through, about 10 minutes. If the meat is still pink in the center, return it to the liquid and cook a minute or two longer. Drain the chicken (save the liquid to use as chicken stock, if you wish). Transfer the chicken to a cutting board. Cut the breast meat off the bone in two single pieces, and discard the bones. Place the chicken meat in a small plastic storage container.

2. To make the sauce, use the flat side of a cleaver or large knife to lightly smash the scallion and ginger. Combine the scallion, ginger, stock, rice wine, salt, and sugar in a small bowl, and stir to dissolve the sugar. Pour the sauce over the chicken. Cover and refrigerate for at least 8 hours or overnight.

3. Drain the chicken. Using a cleaver, chop the chicken into pieces about $1\frac{1}{2}$ inches long and $1/2$ inch wide. Garnish with the cilantro, and serve chilled.

THE SAUCE FOR THIS DISH—thin slices of moist chicken in a sesame sauce served on clear noodles—is identical to the one used for Cold Sesame Noodles. Although you will find both of these excellent dishes listed as cold appetizers at most Chinese restaurants, I personally find them too filling as first courses, and prefer to serve them as entrées at buffets. Do as you please, but keep my advice in mind, or you may be too full to enjoy the rest of your meal.

Makes 2 to 4 servings

Hacked Chicken

1 whole chicken breast with skin and bone (about 1 pound)
1½ ounces bean threads (mung bean flour noodles)

Sauce

1 teaspoon vegetable oil
1 scallion, white part only, trimmed and minced
2 garlic cloves, peeled and minced
2 heaping tablespoons Chinese sesame paste or peanut butter
2 tablespoons Chicken Stock (page 70) or canned chicken broth
1 tablespoon soy sauce
1 tablespoon distilled white vinegar
1 tablespoon rice wine or dry sherry
1 tablespoon sugar
1 teaspoon hot bean paste
1 teaspoon hot chili oil

1 cucumber, peeled, seeded, and cut into thin strips about 1 inch long
2 tablespoons minced cilantro

1. Bring 8 cups of water to a near boil in a medium saucepan over high heat. Add the chicken and cook for 2 minutes. Cover the pot, turn off the heat, and poach the chicken until the meat has turned white and is just cooked through, about 10 minutes. If the meat is still pink in the center, return it to the liquid and cook a minute or two longer. Drain the chicken (save the liquid to use as chicken stock, if you wish). Transfer the chicken to a cutting board and let it cool until easy to handle. Discard the skin

and bones. Following the grain, cut or pull the chicken meat into thick shreds about 1½ inches long and ½ inch wide.

2. Place the bean threads in a medium bowl and add enough hot tap water to cover. Let stand until the threads are tender, 20 minutes.

3. To make the sauce, heat a large wok over high heat. Add the oil. Stir-fry the scallion and garlic until the scallion is wilted, about 20 seconds. Transfer to a medium bowl, add the sesame paste, and mix well. Add the stock, soy sauce, vinegar, rice wine, sugar, hot bean paste, and chili oil, and mix well.

4. Drain the bean threads, and snip them into thirds with kitchen scissors. (This will be approximate—just make them shorter so they are easier to eat.) Place the bean threads on a platter, top with the chicken, and then pour the sesame sauce over the chicken. Garnish with the cucumber and cilantro, and serve.

THIS CRISP SHANGHAINESE PICKLED SALAD, with its mix of hot, sour, and sweet flavors, makes a perfect side dish to rich foods like Braised Duck with Vegetables or Hangzhou Braised Pork. The Shanghainese do not like very spicy foods, so although this has hot peppers and Sichuan peppercorns, the result is gently spicy, not fiery. The cabbage retains its crispness for up to a week if kept refrigerated, which is especially helpful because this recipe makes a large batch.

Makes 4 to 6 servings

Hot and Sour Cabbage

One 2-pound head Napa cabbage
1 tablespoon kosher salt
2 tablespoons vegetable oil
8 small dried hot red chilies
25 Sichuan peppercorns
Dash of dark sesame oil
1 cup sugar
1 cup distilled white vinegar
1 tablespoon hot chili oil
$\frac{1}{4}$ carrot, peeled and cut into thin 2-inch-long strips
One 2-inch piece peeled fresh ginger, cut into thin 2-inch-long strips

1. Cut the leafy top from the cabbage where it meets the thick stem. Reserve the tops for another use. Cut the stems into strips about 4 inches long and $\frac{1}{2}$ inch wide.

2. Place the cabbage strips in a large pan. Dissolve the salt in 1 cup of water, and pour over the cabbage. Place another pan of the same size, or slightly smaller, on top of the cabbage. Add several weights (such as a frying pan or canned goods) on top of the second pan to weight it down, helping to squeeze out as much water as possible from the cabbage. Set aside for 1 to 2 hours, until the cabbage is crisp and has given off a lot of water. Remove the weights and the top pan, and drain the cabbage. In batches, transfer the cabbage to a clean kitchen towel and squeeze out the excess moisture. The cabbage should be quite dry, so that it will stay crisp. Place the cabbage in a plastic storage container.

3. Heat a large wok over high heat. Add the oil, dried chilies, and peppercorns, and stir-fry for 20 seconds. Add the sesame oil, and then immediately pour the mixture through a wire strainer into a small heatproof bowl. Discard the peppers and peppercorns, and pour the seasoned oil over the cabbage. Clean and dry the wok.

4. Place the wok over low heat, and add the sugar and vinegar. Cook, stirring constantly, until the sugar dissolves, about 3 minutes. Pour over the cabbage, and add the chili oil. Sprinkle the carrot and ginger over the cabbage. Cool the cabbage mixture to room temperature. Cover and refrigerate overnight. Serve chilled. (The salad can be stored, covered and refrigerated, for up to 1 week.)

THIS REFRESHING APPETIZER HAS lightly cooked shrimp in a brightly flavored sauce.

Makes 4 servings

Shrimp with Cilantro

12 large shrimp, peeled, deveined, and sliced in half lengthwise
1 tablespoon cornstarch
Pinch of salt

Sauce

1 teaspoon vegetable oil
1 scallion, white part only, trimmed and minced
2 garlic cloves, peeled and minced
$\frac{1}{2}$ teaspoon freshly ground black pepper
1 tablespoon soy sauce
2 teaspoons sugar
2 teaspoons distilled white vinegar
2 teaspoons hot bean paste
1 teaspoon rice wine or dry sherry
1 teaspoon hot chili oil
3 teaspoons minced cilantro

$\frac{1}{4}$ head iceberg lettuce, shredded

1. Combine the shrimp, cornstarch, salt, and 1 tablespoon water in a bowl. Mix well, then rinse the shrimp well under cold running water. Fill a medium bowl with ice water. Bring a medium saucepan of water to a boil over high heat. Add the shrimp to the boiling water and cook just until they turn white, about 20 to 30 seconds. Using a wide wire-mesh strainer, transfer the shrimp to the ice water, where they will curl up into corkscrews. Cool, then drain and pat dry with paper towels. Place the shrimp in a shallow dish.

2. To make the sauce, heat a large wok over high heat. Add the oil, then the scallion, garlic, and black pepper, and stir-fry for 10 to 15 seconds. Transfer to a medium bowl, add the soy sauce, sugar, vinegar, hot bean paste, rice wine, chili oil, and 2 teaspoons of the cilantro, and mix well. Pour the sauce over the shrimp and mix well. Cover, and refrigerate for 30 minutes.

3. Spread the lettuce on a platter and top with the shrimp. Garnish with the remaining 1 teaspoon cilantro, and serve chilled.

THIS SILKEN DISH OF GLISTENING EGGPLANT bathed in a spicy sauce is a cold rendition of the Eggplant with Garlic Sauce on page 218. It is a perfect summer dish or cold appetizer any time of year. Or serve it alongside grilled fish or steak. The eggplant is cooked with an unusual technique. When it is passed through oil, eggplant absorbs the oil like a sponge. To remove some of the oil, it is dropped into boiling water, then drained and patted dry with paper towels.

Makes 4 servings

Sichuan Eggplant

4 small Japanese eggplants (about 1 pound total), trimmed
Vegetable oil, for passing through

Sauce

1 tablespoon vegetable oil
6 garlic cloves, peeled and minced
3 scallions, white part only, trimmed and minced
$1/4$ teaspoon freshly ground black pepper
1 tablespoon dark sesame oil
$1^1/2$ tablespoons distilled white vinegar
1 tablespoon sugar
1 tablespoon soy sauce
1 teaspoon rice wine or dry sherry
1 teaspoon hot bean paste
1 teaspoon hot chili oil

1. Bring a large pot of water to a boil, and keep it at a low boil.

2. Using a sharp knife, lightly score the skin of the eggplants in a crosshatch pattern, with the lines about 1 inch apart. Halve or quarter the eggplants lengthwise to make sticks about $1/2$ inch wide. Cut the sticks into 2-inch lengths.

3. Heat a large wok over high heat. Add enough oil to come about $1^1/2$ inches up the sides of the wok, and heat it to 350°F. Working in batches without crowding, fry the eggplant, turning it occasionally, until tender, about 45 seconds. Do not overcook or it will lose its shape. Using a wide wire-mesh skimmer, quickly remove the fried eggplant

from the oil, dip it briefly in the boiling water, and then transfer it to paper towels to drain. Repeat with the remaining eggplant, drying the skimmer after each use.

4. To make the sauce, heat the 1 tablespoon oil in a small skillet over medium-low heat. Add the garlic and stir-fry until fragrant, about 10 seconds. Add the scallions and black pepper, and stir-fry until the scallions are wilted, about 20 seconds. Add the sesame oil, and transfer the mixture to a bowl. Add the vinegar, sugar, soy sauce, rice wine, hot bean paste, and hot chili oil, and mix well.

5. Place the eggplant on a serving platter and pour the sauce over it. Serve at room temperature.

RAW BEEF IS NOT A TRADITIONAL CHINESE DISH. This hybrid appetizer is similar to Italian carpaccio, with thin slices of raw filet mignon dressed with an intriguing tangy and spicy sauce. I serve this with Scallion Pancakes—the tender meat and perky sauce go well with the crisp, golden cakes. This simple dish takes only 10 minutes to prepare. **Makes 2 to 4 servings**

Tangy Spicy Beef Carpaccio

8 ounces filet mignon, trimmed
1 tablespoon vegetable oil, optional
$\frac{1}{4}$ teaspoon salt
1 cucumber, peeled, cut in half lengthwise, seeded, and then
    sliced diagonally into $\frac{1}{8}$-inch-thick pieces

Sauce

$1\frac{1}{2}$ teaspoons vegetable oil
4 scallions, white part only, trimmed and minced
2 garlic cloves, minced
Pinch of freshly ground black pepper
1 tablespoon distilled white vinegar
2 teaspoons hot bean paste
2 teaspoons rice wine or dry sherry
1 teaspoon hot chili oil
1 teaspoon soy sauce
$\frac{1}{4}$ teaspoon sugar

4 cilantro sprigs, minced

1. Cut the filet mignon in half horizontally. (If you wish, the filet mignon can also be seared, then sliced. Heat the 1 tablespoon vegetable oil in a skillet over high heat until smoking. Add the filet and cook on each side for 1 minute. It will be very rare, although the outside will be browned. Transfer to a cutting board.) Cut each half across the grain into pieces $1\frac{1}{2}$ inches long, 1 inch wide, and $\frac{1}{8}$ inch thick.

2. Sprinkle the salt over the cucumber slices, and set aside for 5 minutes. Then squeeze the excess moisture from the cucumber. Place the cucumber slices, overlapping, on a platter. Arrange the sliced beef on top of the cucumber, overlapping the slices of beef.

3. To make the sauce, heat a wok over high heat. Add the oil, then the scallions, garlic, and black pepper, and stir-fry for 20 seconds. Transfer the scallion mixture to a medium bowl. Add the vinegar, hot bean paste, rice wine, hot chili oil, soy sauce, and sugar, and mix well to dissolve the sugar. Pour the sauce over the beef. Garnish with the cilantro, and serve immediately.

IN THE SHANGHAI DIALECT, yo-pao means "going through oil." The shrimp, sliced almost in half, puff dramatically in their shells when quickly passed through the hot oil. A brief stir-fry in a gingery, sweet sauce finishes the dish.

Makes 4 servings

Yo-Pao Shrimp

12 jumbo shrimp in their shells
Vegetable oil, for passing through
$1/3$ cup ketchup
1 tablespoon plus 1 teaspoon rice wine or dry sherry
1 tablespoon plus 1 teaspoon sugar
$1/4$ teaspoon salt
4 scallions, white part only, trimmed and sliced diagonally into 1-inch pieces
Eight $1/8$-inch-thick slices peeled fresh ginger, cut into thin $1 1/2$-inch-long strips

1. Using kitchen scissors, snip along the back of each shrimp shell. Devein the shrimp and remove any feelers, keeping the shell attached. Using a paring knife, cut deeper into the deveining incision, slicing almost, but not completely, through the shrimp. (This is called butterflying the shrimp.)

2. Heat a large wok over high heat. Add enough oil to come about 2 inches up the sides of the wok, and heat it to 375°F. Add the shrimp and fry until the they open up and turn white, about 30 to 40 seconds. Using a wide wire-mesh strainer, transfer the shrimp to a colander to drain. Discard all but 2 tablespoons of the oil.

3. In a small bowl, mix the ketchup, rice wine, sugar, and salt. Return the wok with the oil to high heat. Add the scallions and ginger and stir-fry until the scallions are wilted, about 20 seconds. Stir in the ketchup mixture. Add the shrimp, and stir-fry to coat them with the sauce. Transfer to a serving plate and cool to room temperature.

Soups

*I*N CHINA, most families have soup with their meals. Until recently drinks—tea, water, beer, or wine—were not served with a family dinner, so the soup was not just a savory dish but also the liquid refreshment. The Cantonese start their meal with soup, while the people of Beijing and Shanghai have soup during the course of the meal. At a banquet, soup is served in the middle or at the end, not at the beginning.

Today it is more common to serve beer or wine with a meal at home, and of course people do drink alcoholic beverages when dining at restaurants.

A soup can be thin and clear, or thick and filled with meat, noodles, or dumplings. At Shun Lee, most of our customers enjoy their soup as an appetizer, or perhaps someone will order one of the more substantial soups for their lunchtime meal.

Soup-making is a satisfying experience, especially if you make your own stock. A soup like Velvet Chicken and Corn Soup takes only ten minutes, while the rich, fragrant West Lake Duck Soup simmers for several hours.

CHICKEN STOCK IS USED IN COOKING many Chinese dishes, whether meat, fowl, fish, or vegetable. Shun Lee's everyday chicken stock, which we make fresh each day, is light and clean-tasting. It is worth making because it is excellent, and because it keeps well in the freezer. You can use canned reduced-sodium chicken broth in a pinch, but it is seasoned for Western dishes, not Asian ones. Nonetheless, it is an acceptable substitute. **Makes 2 quarts**

Chicken Stock

One $3^1/_2$-pound whole chicken, chopped with a cleaver into 16 to 20 pieces
3 scallions, white and green parts, trimmed and flattened with the cleaver
Five $^1/_8$-inch-thick slices peeled fresh ginger
One 4-ounce piece Smithfield ham, cut into 12 pieces

1. Bring a large saucepan of water to a boil over high heat. Add the chicken and cook for about $1^1/_2$ minutes to remove some of the surface fat. Drain, and rinse under cold running water. (This refreshes the chicken.)

2. Return the chicken to the saucepan. Add 12 cups of water and the scallions, ginger, and ham. Bring to a boil over high heat. Reduce the heat to low and partially cover the saucepan. Simmer until deeply flavored, about $1^1/_2$ hours.

3. Using a wide wire-mesh skimmer, remove and discard the solids from the stock. Strain the stock through a fine-mesh wire sieve into a large bowl. Cool until tepid. Cover and refrigerate until chilled, at least 4 hours or overnight.

4. Scrape off and discard the yellow fat from the surface of the stock. Store the stock, covered and refrigerated, for up to 5 days, or freeze it in an airtight container for up to 1 month.

THIS FAMOUS SOUP, brimming with morsels of bean curd, dried lilies, and tree ears, is popular in Beijing, Shanghai, and Chengdu. In Beijing, people often make a complete meal of the soup, accompanying it with either scallion pancakes or pan-fried dumplings, and I suggest that you might do the same. **Makes 4 servings**

Hot and Sour Soup

$\frac{1}{2}$ cup (1$\frac{1}{2}$ ounces) tree ears

$\frac{1}{4}$ cup (1 ounce) dried lily buds

4 Chinese dried black mushrooms (1$\frac{1}{2}$ ounces)

2 ounces boneless, skinless chicken breast,
    cut into thin 1-inch-long strips

$\frac{1}{4}$ cup canned bamboo shoots (1$\frac{1}{2}$ ounces), rinsed, drained, and
    cut into 1-inch-long julienne

$\frac{1}{2}$ cake firm bean curd, cut in half horizontally, and
    then crosswise into thin 1-inch-long strips

1 large egg

1 tablespoon vegetable oil

4 cups Chicken Stock (page 70) or canned chicken broth

$\frac{1}{4}$ cup soy sauce

1$\frac{1}{2}$ teaspoons ground white pepper, or more to taste

$\frac{1}{4}$ cup cornstarch

$\frac{1}{4}$ cup distilled white vinegar

1 tablespoon dark sesame oil

1 scallion, green part only, trimmed and minced

1. Place the tree ears, lily buds, and dried mushrooms in three separate bowls. Add hot water to cover to each bowl, and let stand until the vegetables have softened, about 30 minutes. Drain, and cut each vegetable into thin 1-inch-long strips. Set aside.

2. Bring a large saucepan of water to a boil over high heat. Add the chicken, bamboo shoots, bean curd, tree ears, lilies, and mushrooms, and cook until the chicken turns opaque, about 30 seconds. Drain in a colander. Clean the saucepan.

3. Beat the egg in a small bowl until frothy. Heat the oil in an 8-inch nonstick skillet over medium-low heat. Drizzle in the beaten egg to make a thin, lacy crepe, and cook

until set, about 1 minute. Slide the crepe gently out of the skillet onto a cutting board, and slice it into $\frac{1}{4}$-inch thick shreds about 2 inches long.

4. Bring the stock, soy sauce, and white pepper to a boil in a large saucepan over medium heat. Add the drained chicken mixture and return to a boil.

5. Dissolve the cornstarch in $\frac{1}{2}$ cup cold water in a small bowl. Add to the saucepan, and stir gently until the soup thickens, about 30 seconds. Taste the soup, and add more white pepper if you wish. The soup should be spicy, but season it gradually or you may go too far. Transfer the soup to a large serving bowl, and stir in the vinegar and sesame oil. Garnish with the egg strips and scallion, and serve immediately.

THIS FRAGRANT SOUP, a Shun Lee original, is an improvisation on Thai hot and sour shrimp soup. We combined the basics of French bouillabaisse, a seafood-laden soup with lots of shellfish and fish, with Thai flavors. The soup is fast-cooking, and when served with a salad, makes a complete meal. The broth is light, yet complex and tangy. The secret is not to overcook the seafood. Have your fishmonger cut up a live lobster for you, and use it within a few hours of purchase.

Only a small amount of the Tom Yum Hot and Sour Soup Base is used; the rest can be frozen.   **Makes 4 servings**

Hot and Sour Bouillabaisse

Stock

One 1$\frac{1}{2}$-pound lobster, uncooked: claws chopped in half,
   and the tail chopped lengthwise and then in half crosswise
8 medium shrimp
2 tablespoons Chinese dried baby shrimp
Two $\frac{1}{4}$-inch-thick slices galangal, unpeeled and smashed under a cleaver
Two $\frac{1}{4}$-inch-thick slices peeled fresh ginger, smashed under a cleaver
1 medium red onion, peeled and cut into 6 equal wedges
1 medium white onion, peeled and cut into 6 equal wedges
$\frac{1}{2}$ tomato, cut into 4 equal wedges
$\frac{1}{2}$ red bell pepper, seeded and cut into thirds
3 Thai or Serrano chilies, seeds and ribs removed, smashed under a cleaver
1 lemongrass stalk, outer peel and tough tops cut off and discarded,
   tender bulb cut in half lengthwise and smashed
$\frac{1}{2}$ teaspoon salt

1 teaspoon sugar
2 tablespoons distilled white vinegar
1$\frac{1}{2}$ teaspoons Thai Kitchen Tom Yum Hot and Sour Soup Base (see Note)
4 ounces skinless sea bass fillet, cut into 4 pieces, each about
   2 inches square and $\frac{1}{2}$ inch thick
8 littleneck clams, scrubbed
2 scallops, each sliced in half horizontally
Juice of $\frac{1}{2}$ lime
8 basil leaves

1. To make the soup stock, bring a large saucepan of water to a boil over high heat. Add the lobster and cook until the shell turns red, 3 to 4 minutes. Drain in a colander and let stand until cool enough to handle. Crack the lobster and remove the meat, saving the shell. Clean the saucepan. Set the meat and shell aside separately.

2. Peel and devein the shrimp, reserving the shells. Refrigerate the cleaned shrimp.

3. Bring 4 cups of water to a boil in the saucepan over high heat. Add the lobster shells and shrimp shells, along with the dried baby shrimp, galangal, ginger, red and white onions, tomato, bell pepper, chilies, lemongrass, and salt. Return to a boil. Reduce the heat to medium-low and simmer, uncovered, for 15 minutes. Strain the stock into a bowl and discard the shells and vegetables.

4. Return the stock to the saucepan. Add the sugar, vinegar, and Tom Yum Hot and Sour Soup Base, and increase the heat to high. Add the shrimp, sea bass, clams, scallops, and lime juice. Cook until the clams open, about 2 minutes. Add the lobster meat and heat for 30 seconds. Discard any unopened clams.

5. Place the basil leaves in a serving bowl. Using a slotted spoon, transfer the seafood to the serving bowl. Strain the broth through a wire fine-mesh strainer over the seafood. Serve immediately.

Note: Thai Kitchen Tom Yum Hot and Sour Soup Base, which is an excellent blend of many Thai ingredients, can be ordered from www.pacificrim-gourmet.com.

A BOWL OF PLUMP WONTONS FLOATING IN BROTH is the single most popular snack throughout China. It can be eaten as a complete meal for breakfast or lunch, as a child's after-school snack, or as a late-night repast. It is also a very common street food, sold at outdoor stands from early morning to midnight. Our Shanghai Wonton Soup is an exceptionally pretty rendition, with shreds of a lacy egg crepe, seaweed, and some optional bok choy adrift in the broth.

Makes 4 servings

Shanghai Wonton Soup

Wontons

$3/4$ cup (2 ounces) coarsely chopped baby bok choy or Napa cabbage

2 ounces boneless, skinless chicken breast, coarsely chopped

5 ounces pork butt, coarsely chopped

2 ounces medium shrimp, peeled and deveined, coarsely chopped

1 scallion, trimmed, white and green parts separated, and minced

1 tablespoon vegetable oil

1 teaspoon dark sesame oil

$1/2$ teaspoon salt

1 large egg white

Cornstarch, for the waxed paper

20 wonton skins

Soup

1 large egg

1 tablespoon vegetable oil

1 sheet roasted seaweed (nori)

1 tablespoon ($1/2$ ounce) minced Sichuan preserved vegetable, rinsed and drained

4 cups Chicken Stock (page 70) or canned chicken broth

$1/2$ teaspoon salt

1. To make the wonton filling, pulse the bok choy in a food processor until minced. Transfer to a bowl. Separately pulse the chicken, pork, and shrimp in the food processor until minced, and add to the bok choy. Add the white part of the scallion, oil, sesame oil, and salt, and mix well.

2. Beat the egg white in a small bowl until frothy. Line a baking sheet with waxed paper and dust it with cornstarch. Using a knife or a teaspoon, place a teaspoonful of the

chicken mixture in the middle of a wonton skin. Dip your finger in the egg white, and moisten the edges of the skin. Fold the wonton skin in half, from top to bottom, and seal the edges with egg white. Bring the sides of the wrapper toward you, and overlap the bottom corners by about 1/2 inch. Pinch the wrapper so that the corners adhere to each other, and seal with egg white. Place on the baking sheet. Repeat with the remaining filling and wonton skins. (The uncooked wontons can be made up to 1 day ahead, covered, and refrigerated. Or freeze them for up to 2 weeks. To freeze, place them in a single layer in a plastic storage container or plastic storage bag, arranged so that the wontons don't touch one another. When you are ready to cook them, the frozen wontons will be easy to remove, one by one.)

3. To make the soup, beat the egg in a small bowl until frothy. Heat the oil in an 8-inch nonstick skillet over medium heat. Drizzle in the egg to make a thin, lacy crepe and cook until set, about 1 minute. Slide it gently onto a cutting board, let it cool, and cut it into shreds.

4. Tear the roasted seaweed into rough-edged 2-inch squares. Place the egg strips, seaweed, green part of the scallion, and preserved vegetable in a big serving bowl. Bring the stock and salt to a boil in a large saucepan over high heat; then turn the heat to low.

5. Bring 8 cups of water to a boil in a large pot over high heat. Add the wontons and return to a boil. Add 1/2 cup cold water, and return to a boil again. Add a final 1/2 cup cold water, and return to a boil once more. (Adding the water slows the cooking, helping the wontons to keep their shape.)

6. Using a slotted spoon, transfer the wontons to the serving bowl. Pour the hot stock over the wontons, and serve immediately.

WHEN A CHINESE WOMAN has to feed her family and doesn't have much food in the house, she cracks open some eggs, adds some broth, steams the mixture, and produces a delicate custard-like soup. We have embellished this dish by adding clams, mushrooms, tomatoes, and peas. It can also be garnished with a little soy sauce and minced scallions and spooned over rice. You can substitute small shrimp or chopped scallops for the clams.   **Makes 4 servings**

Steamed Egg Custard Soup with Clams

8 littleneck clams, shucked, shells discarded

2 large eggs

1 teaspoon rice wine or dry sherry

3 cups Chicken Stock (page 70) or canned chicken broth,
   cold or at cool room temperature (see Note)

1 tablespoon cornstarch

4 Chinese dried black mushrooms, soaked until softened, trimmed and diced

1 tablespoon thawed frozen baby green peas

1 small plum tomato, skinned, seeded, and chopped

2 teaspoons oyster sauce

1 teaspoon dark sesame oil

Pinch of ground white pepper

1. Place about 1 inch of water in the bottom of an Asian-style steamer, and bring it to a boil over high heat. Place the clams in a 9-inch-diameter, 3-inch-deep heatproof bowl.

2. Beat the eggs in a medium bowl until combined. Then beat in the rice wine. Beat in 2 cups of the stock, and pour over the clams. Place the heatproof bowl in the steamer, cover, and steam until the custard is set, 12 to 14 minutes. Turn off the heat, set the steamer lid ajar, and let stand to keep the custard warm.

3. Dissolve the cornstarch in 2 tablespoons water in a small bowl. Bring the remaining 1 cup stock to a boil in a medium saucepan. Stir in the cornstarch mixture, along with the mushrooms, peas, tomatoes, oyster sauce, sesame oil, and white pepper. Stir until heated through.

4. Remove the bowl of custard from the steamer. Run a dull knife around the inside edge of the bowl, and invert the bowl into a large serving bowl to unmold the custard. Pour the vegetable mixture around the custard, and serve immediately.

Note: The chicken stock must be cold or no warmer than room temperature. If at all warm, it could cook the eggs too soon and make an ugly, messy, clotted custard.

THIS WARMING SOUP is a famous dish from Hangzhou. This is how we make it at Shun Lee, with a base stock that uses a whole chicken (which is discarded, making it a particularly extravagant dish) and a small, young wild duck or a Moulard wild duck. If you can't find a small wild duck, make the variation that uses the larger Muscovy ducks found in supermarkets. **Makes 4 to 6 servings**

West Lake Duck Soup

One 3-pound chicken, cut into 4 pieces
$\frac{1}{3}$ cup rice wine or dry sherry
1 scallion, white and green parts, trimmed
One 4-inch-long piece peeled fresh ginger, cut into 8 equal pieces,
    and smashed under a cleaver
$\frac{1}{2}$ cup (4 ounces) dried bamboo shoots
One 2$\frac{1}{2}$-pound wild duck
8 baby bok choy
4 ounces Smithfield ham, cut into pieces 2 inches long, 1 inch wide, and $\frac{1}{4}$ inch thick

Dipping sauce
    $\frac{1}{2}$ cup Chinese black or balsamic vinegar
    3 tablespoons soy sauce

1. Pour 3 quarts of water into a large pot that will hold both the chicken and the duck, and bring to a boil over high heat. Add the chicken, rice wine, scallion, and ginger. Bring back to a boil, reduce the heat to medium-low, and partially cover. Simmer for 1 hour.

2. Meanwhile, place the bamboo shoots in a bowl and add hot tap water to cover. Let stand until softened, about 15 minutes. Drain well. Cut the shoots into $\frac{1}{4}$-inch-thick strips about 4 inches long. Set aside.

3. Bring another large pot of water to a boil over high heat. Add the duck and boil for 30 seconds to remove some of the surface fat. Drain the duck and rinse it under cold running water.

4. Add the duck to the stock, arranging the duck on the bottom and the chicken pieces on top. Return to a boil, and add the bamboo shoots. Partially cover the pot, allowing a

small bit of air to escape. Lower the heat to medium-low and simmer until the duck is tender, about 2 hours. Be sure that the stock never goes beyond a steady simmer and that the pot is not tightly covered, or the fat will be difficult to remove later.

5. Remove the chicken from the stock, and discard or use for another purpose. Skim the surface of the stock of as much fat as possible. Add the bok choy, and place the ham on top of the duck. If the level of stock has noticeably lowered, replace it with the equivalent amount of boiling water. Return the stock to a boil, and cook until the bok choy is crisp-tender, about 1 minute. Transfer the soup to a tureen.

6. To serve the soup, mix the vinegar with the soy sauce in a small bowl, remove the duck from the stock and place it on a serving platter. Using chopsticks, each person pulls the meat off in pieces, and puts the meat on their plate. For each serving, place a portion of the duck meat in a soup bowl, and ladle in the soup and vegetables. Serve hot, with the vinegar mixture as a dip for the duck meat that is not in the soup.

West Lake Duck Soup with Dumplings: The addition of dumplings makes this soup even more substantial. Served with a vegetable side dish, such as Buddha's Delight (page 209), it makes a complete meal. And as the dumplings look a bit like eggs, they play up the poultry mother-hen (or mother-duck) connection. Make Sichuan Boiled Dumplings (page 47), and boil them in water until cooked. Drain the dumplings and add a few to each serving of the soup.

West Lake Muscovy Duck Soup: Substitute one 5-pound Muscovy or Moulard duck, cut into 4 pieces, for the chicken and wild duck. Substitute 2 quarts Chicken Stock (page 70) and 1 quart water for the water in step 1; simmer the scallion, ginger, and rice wine for 30 minutes. Continue as directed, substituting the Muscovy duck for the wild duck in step 3.

THIS GENTLE, SOOTHING SOUP flecked with tiny, tender bits of chicken, along with corn, peas, and strands of egg white, is a fusion dish that Hong Kong chefs created with Western ingredients.

Makes 4 servings

Velvet Chicken and Corn Soup

3 ounces boneless, skinless chicken breast,
  minced in a food processor or with a cleaver
$1/3$ cup minced water chestnuts
4 cups Chicken Stock (page 70) or canned chicken broth
Two $14 1/2$-ounce cans cream-style corn
$1/2$ teaspoon salt, plus more to taste
$1/4$ teaspoon sugar
2 tablespoons cornstarch
$1/4$ cup thawed frozen baby green peas
2 large egg whites
1 scallion, green and white parts, trimmed and minced

1. Bring 2 cups of water to a boil in a medium saucepan over high heat. Add the chicken and water chestnuts, and stir until the chicken turns white, about 10 seconds. Drain the chicken and water chestnuts in a large fine-mesh strainer.

2. In a large pot, bring the chicken stock to a boil. Add the creamed corn, salt, and sugar, and stir until well blended. Return to a boil.

3. Dissolve the cornstarch in $1/4$ cup cold water in a small bowl. Beat the egg whites in a small bowl until foamy. Add the chicken and water chestnuts to the stock. Stir in the cornstarch mixture and cook until the soup thickens slightly, about 10 seconds. Stirring constantly, drizzle the egg white into the soup, so that the egg white turns into strands. Add the peas. Season with more salt, if desired. Garnish with the scallion and serve immediately.

THIS SOUP IS STEAMED SLOWLY for 2 hours, melding the sweet flavor of the chicken with the salty-sweet taste of cured ham. In China, where every province has its own specialties, some dishes seldom stray beyond the borders. This soup is an example—it is usually served only in Yunnan restaurants. You will need a large heatproof ceramic bowl with a lid to hold the chicken and the stock. They are easily found at Asian markets, which often have a housewares department. In order to remove all traces of fat from the broth, make the soup a day ahead and refrigerate it so the fat can solidify and be lifted off. **Makes 4 to 6 servings**

Yunnan Steamed Chicken Soup

2 pounds chicken breasts or thighs, chopped through the bones into 16 to 20 pieces
$1\frac{1}{2}$ ounces Smithfield ham, cut into pieces 1 inch long, $\frac{1}{2}$ inch wide, and $\frac{1}{4}$ inch thick
One 1-inch piece peeled fresh ginger, sliced $\frac{1}{4}$ inch thick and cut into $\frac{1}{2}$-inch pieces
4 cups Chicken Stock (page 70) or canned chicken broth
1 teaspoon rice wine or dry sherry
$\frac{1}{2}$ teaspoon salt

1. Bring a large pot of water to a boil over high heat. Add the chicken and cook for about $1\frac{1}{2}$ minutes to remove excess surface fat. Drain in a colander and rinse under cold running water. Place the chicken in a large ceramic bowl with a lid (for example, a 9-inch-diameter, 3-inch-deep bowl), and add the ham and ginger.

2. Add about 2 inches of water to the bottom of an Asian-style steamer, and bring it to a boil over high heat.

3. Bring the stock, rice wine, and salt to a boil in a large saucepan over high heat. Pour over the chicken in the bowl. Cover the bowl tightly with a lid, then plastic wrap. Place the wrapped bowl in the steamer and cover. Reduce the heat to medium-low and steam at a brisk simmer for 2 hours. Periodically add boiling water to the steamer to keep a good head of steam.

4. Carefully remove the bowl from the steamer. Uncover the bowl and let cool to room temperature. Cover it again, and refrigerate for 12 hours or overnight.

5. Skim off the solidified fat from the surface of the broth. Transfer the soup to a large saucepan and reheat to simmering. Serve immediately.

Fish and Shellfish

IN MANDARIN, the sound of the word for "fish," *yu,* also means "surplus"—that you will never lack for anything. The fish, then, is a symbol of prosperity, and it is always served at birthdays, weddings, and anniversaries.

The Chinese prefer freshwater fish, like pike and carp, because the meat is more tender and flakier than that of ocean fish, but they also eat saltwater fish like sea bass, grouper, and flounder. They prefer their fish small, rather than large, because they believe that smaller fish have more delicate meat. If two people are sharing a whole fish, they will buy or order a one-pound fish. If four people are sharing a fish, they may order two one-pound fish instead of a single two-pound fish. The Cantonese steam fish to retain the sparklingly fresh flavor and texture, while the Shanghainese braise fish in soy sauce and sugar to create a more richly flavored dish. In Sichuan, people braise their fish with lots of chilies and Sichuan peppercorns. Regardless of how the Chinese cook their fish, they prefer to buy only live fish.

THIS BEIJING DISH IS DELICATE IN COLOR, texture, and flavor. The thin squares of fish are cooked for only a few seconds, so they remain milky-white and tender. The silken fish contrasts with the crispness of the snow peas and the water chestnuts, and also with the subtle crunch of the tree ear mushrooms.

Makes 4 servings

Heavenly Fish Fillet

12 ounces skinless sea bass fillet, cut into pieces $2\frac{1}{2}$ inches long and 1 inch wide

$\frac{1}{2}$ large egg white (beat a whole egg white until foamy and measure out half)

3 teaspoons cornstarch

$\frac{1}{2}$ cup (2 ounces) snow peas

4 water chestnuts, each cut into 3 slices

$\frac{1}{3}$ cup tree ears, soaked in hot tap water until softened, drained

Vegetable oil, for passing through

1 scallion, white part only, trimmed and minced

1 teaspoon peeled and minced fresh ginger

$\frac{1}{3}$ cup Chicken Stock (page 70), canned chicken broth, or fish stock

3 tablespoons rice wine or dry sherry

1 tablespoon sugar

$\frac{1}{2}$ teaspoon salt

1. Gently mix the fish, egg white, and 1 teaspoon of the cornstarch in a medium bowl until thoroughly combined.

2. Bring a medium saucepan of lightly salted water to a boil over high heat. Add the snow peas, water chestnuts, and tree ears, and cook for 10 seconds. Drain in a colander.

3. Heat a large wok over high heat. Add enough oil to come 1 inch up the sides of the wok, and heat it to 300°F. Quickly add the fish, one piece at a time. Stirring gently to keep the fish in motion, cook just until it turns white, about 1 minute. Using a wide wire-mesh strainer, transfer the fish to a colander to drain.

4. Discard all but 2 tablespoons of the oil from the wok. Return the wok with the oil to high heat. Add the scallion and ginger, and stir-fry for 10 seconds. Add the stock, rice wine, sugar, and salt, and bring to a boil. Dissolve the remaining 2 teaspoons cornstarch in 2 tablespoons cold water, and add to the wok. Return the fish to the wok, and add the snow peas, water chestnuts, and tree ears. Stir gently until the sauce thickens, about 20 seconds, being sure not to break up the fish. Serve immediately.

THIS IS ONE OF MY FAVORITE WAYS to prepare a whole fresh fish: poached, with a sauce drizzled over it at the last moment. Poaching is an ancient cooking technique that is also perfect for people who want low-carb, low-fat dishes. Here it results in a silken fish that isn't overcooked. **Makes 4 servings**

Poached Sea Bass Cantonese

One 2-pound sea bass, scaled and cleaned, with head and tail intact
4 scallions, white and green parts, trimmed
Three $1/8$-inch-thick slices peeled fresh ginger
$1/4$ cup rice wine or dry sherry

$1/4$ cup vegetable oil
$1/4$ cup soy sauce
1 teaspoon sugar
6 scallions, trimmed, white and green parts separated and cut into
    thin 2-inch-long strips (1 cup)
Six $1/8$-inch-thick slices peeled fresh ginger, cut into thin strips
6 cilantro sprigs

1. Bring 10 cups of water to a boil in a large wok over high heat. Starting right behind the gill, make five evenly spaced cuts on each side of the fish, cutting down to, but not through, the bone (this will help the fish cook evenly).

2. Holding the fish by the tail, slide it gently down the side of the wok into the boiling water. Cover the wok, and return the water to a boil for 10 seconds. Turn off the heat, uncover the wok, and add the whole scallions, sliced ginger, and rice wine. Cover again, and let the fish stand in the hot water until the flesh flakes easily from the bone when prodded gently with a chopstick, about 7 minutes. If necessary, cover again and let the fish stand for another few minutes until the flesh flakes.

3. Meanwhile, heat the oil in a small saucepan over high heat until it shimmers. Mix the soy sauce and sugar in a small bowl.

4. To serve, use two spatulas or shallow scoops to transfer the fish to a platter. Sprinkle the white scallions strips over the fish, then sprinkle with the green strips and the ginger strips. Pour the hot oil over the fish, and then drizzle with the soy sauce mixture. Garnish with the cilantro, and serve immediately.

AT SHUN LEE, we serve a dish that is similar to this, where the salmon is sautéed in such a manner that makes the fillet look as if it were wrapped in scallions. This version has the same ingredients, requires no special techniques, and tastes just as good.

Makes 4 servings

Salmon Fillet with Scallions

$1/3$ cup plus 2 tablespoons vegetable oil
1 pound skinless salmon fillet, cut into 4 pieces
$1/4$ cup rice wine or dry sherry
3 tablespoons double black soy sauce, preferably Koon Chun, or regular soy sauce
2 tablespoons sugar
1 teaspoon dark sesame oil
1 tablespoon cornstarch
6 scallions, trimmed and sliced diagonally into $1/1_2$-inch pieces
2 tablespoons peeled and chopped fresh ginger ($1/4$-inch dice)
$1/4$ teaspoon ground white pepper

1. Heat a large wok over high heat. Add the $1/3$ cup vegetable oil and heat until it is hot but not shimmering, about 1 minute. Gently slide the salmon pieces into the wok from the side, so the oil doesn't splash. Fry the fish for 30 seconds on one side; then turn it over and fry for 30 seconds more for medium-rare. (For medium doneness, cook the fish for 40 seconds on each side.) Using a wide wire-mesh skimmer, transfer the fish to paper towels to drain. Discard the oil and wipe out the wok with paper towels.

2. Mix the rice wine, soy sauce, sugar, and sesame oil in a small bowl until blended. Dissolve the cornstarch in 3 tablespoons cold water in another small bowl. Set both bowls aside.

3. Add the remaining 2 tablespoons vegetable oil to the wok, and heat it over high heat until the oil shimmers. Add the scallions and ginger, and stir-fry until the scallions wilt, about 1 minute. Stir in the rice wine mixture.

4. Return the fish to the wok and add the white pepper. Add the cornstarch mixture and gently stir-fry until the sauce thickens, about 20 seconds.

5. Using a slotted spoon, transfer the fish to a serving platter. Spoon the sauce over all. Serve immediately.

IN SHANGHAI, this festive-looking dish is also known as the "squirrel fish," because when the deep-fried fish puffs up, it has a vague resemblance to a squirrel's fluffy tail. It is brilliantly colored, glistening with a crimson sweet and sour sauce, and studded with lychees and loquats.   **Makes 4 servings**

Sweet-and-Sour Whole Crispy Red Snapper

Vegetable oil, for passing through
One 2-pound red snapper, scaled and cleaned, with head and tail intact
1 tablespoon rice wine or dry sherry
Pinch of salt
1 cup cornstarch, for coating the fish

Sauce
$^3/_4$ cup ketchup
1 cup distilled white vinegar
1 cup sugar
$^1/_4$ cup cornstarch
1 red onion, peeled and cut into $^1/_2$-inch dice
5 whole pitted canned lychees
5 whole pitted canned loquats
$^1/_2$ red bell pepper, seeds and ribs removed, cut into $^1/_2$-inch dice
$^1/_4$ cup rice wine or dry sherry
$^1/_2$ teaspoon salt
$^1/_2$ cup thawed frozen baby green peas
2 tablespoons vegetable oil

$^1/_4$ cup toasted pine nuts (see page 28), for garnish

1. Heat a large wok over high heat. Add enough vegetable oil to come about 2 inches up the sides of the wok, and heat it to 375°F. While the oil is heating, prepare the fish: Starting right behind the gill, make four evenly spaced cuts on each side of the fish, cutting down to, but not through, the bone (this will help the fish cook evenly).

2. Sprinkle the fish with the rice wine and the pinch of salt. Spread the cornstarch on a baking sheet or platter. Holding the fish by the tail, dip it in the cornstarch, coating

it thoroughly. When the oil is ready, hold the fish by the tail and slide it gently into the wok, lowering it head-first down the side of the wok so the oil doesn't splash. The oil should bubble in a lively fashion. Fry the fish on one side until golden and crispy, 3 to 4 minutes. The fish slices will begin to separate and puff up. Turn the fish over, and fry the other side until golden and crispy, about 3 to 4 minutes.

3. While the fish is frying, begin the sauce. Mix the ketchup, vinegar, sugar, and $\frac{1}{2}$ cup water in a medium bowl, stirring to dissolve the sugar. Mix well. Heat a small saucepan over high heat. Add the ketchup mixture and stir for 30 seconds; set it aside. Dissolve the cornstarch in $\frac{1}{2}$ cup cold water in a small bowl, and set it aside.

4. Using a wide wire-mesh strainer, transfer the fish to a wire cake rack set over a rimmed baking sheet. Discard all but 2 tablespoons of the oil from the wok. Place the fish on its belly on a platter. Using a kitchen towel, cover the top of the fish and press firmly and gently to balance the fish on its belly. Remove the towel.

5. Return the wok with the oil to high heat. Add the onion and stir-fry for 10 seconds. Add the lychees, loquats, and bell pepper, and stir-fry until the pepper is crisp-tender, about 1 minute. Add the ketchup mixture and bring to a boil. Add the rice wine and salt, then the cornstarch mixture. Add the peas and stir for 10 seconds. Stir in the vegetable oil (to smooth the sauce), and cook for 10 seconds more. Pour the sauce over the fish. Sprinkle with the toasted pine nuts, and serve immediately.

IN THE 1940S, a lobster dish called Lobster Cantonese, unlike anything ever seen in Canton, was popular on the menus of New York's Chinese restaurants. With its gooey, eggy sauce, it was never one of my favorites. My version, introduced at Shun Lee in 1980, utilizes the true flavors of Cantonese cooking and allows the sweetness of the lobster to sing out. **Makes 4 servings**

Lobster Cantonese with Black Beans

One 1$\frac{1}{2}$-pound uncooked lobster, cut into 12 pieces,
    each piece cracked (see Note)
3 tablespoons cornstarch
Vegetable oil, for passing through

Sauce
    1$\frac{1}{2}$ tablespoons soy sauce
    2 tablespoons rice wine or dry sherry
    2 teaspoons sugar
    3 scallions, white parts trimmed and sliced into $\frac{1}{2}$-inch pieces,
        green parts trimmed and sliced into 2-inch pieces
    1 tablespoon peeled and minced fresh ginger
    3 garlic cloves, peeled and very thinly sliced
    30 Chinese fermented black beans, lightly crushed with a cleaver and minced
    $\frac{1}{2}$ teaspoon dark sesame oil

1. Toss the lobster with the cornstarch in a medium bowl (this will seal the meat and help keep it tender). Heat a large wok over high heat. Add enough oil to come 1 inch up the sides of the wok, and heat it to 325°F. In batches without crowding, add the lobster and stir gently until the shells turn bright red, about 1 to 1$\frac{1}{2}$ minutes. Using a wide wire-mesh strainer, transfer the lobster to a colander. Discard all but 2 tablespoons of the oil from the wok.

2. To begin the sauce, mix the soy sauce, rice wine, and sugar in a small bowl, stirring to dissolve the sugar. Set it aside.

3. Return the wok with the oil to high heat. Add the white scallion pieces along with the ginger, garlic, and black beans. Stir-fry for 10 seconds. Add the lobster, then the

soy sauce mixture. Stir-fry for 45 seconds. Add the green scallion pieces, and stir-fry until the sauce is glossy and the lobster is cooked through, about 45 seconds. Add the sesame oil. Serve immediately.

Note: To get 12 pieces of lobster, use a heavy cleaver to chop the body into 4 pieces, the tail into 2 pieces, and the claws into 3 pieces each. Crack the pieces of lobster. Cover and refrigerate until ready to use. If you wish, have your fishmonger do this. Use the lobster within a few hours of chopping it up.

THE PRISTINELY WHITE LOBSTER TAIL and the silken fried egg white are studded with bits of color—green sugar snap peas, red bell pepper, and black tree ears. This was created as a Chinese banquet dish, but it is an excellent dinner party entrée too, as the lobster tails make a very elegant presentation.

Makes 2 to 3 servings

Snow White Lobster Tail

6 thawed frozen lobster tails
1 large egg white
1 tablespoon cornstarch
Pinch of salt
1 teaspoon vegetable oil

Sauce

2 tablespoons Chicken Stock (page 70) or canned chicken broth
1 tablespoon rice wine or dry sherry
1 teaspoon salt
1 teaspoon sugar
Pinch of ground white pepper
1 teaspoon cornstarch
Vegetable oil, for passing through
6 large egg whites
$3/4$ cup (3 ounces) sugar snap peas, trimmed
1 red bell pepper, seeds and ribs discarded, cut into 1-inch squares
2 scallions, white part only, sliced diagonally into 1-inch pieces
Three $1/8$-inch-thick slices of peeled fresh ginger,
    cut into thin $1\frac{1}{2}$-inch-long strips
$1/2$ cup (2 ounces) tree ears, soaked in hot tap water to cover
    until softened, drained and cut in half

1. Using kitchen shears, cut the lobster shells down the middle and remove the meat. Trim off and discard the reddish part so that the lobster meat is all white. Rinse the lobster meat under cold running water and pat it dry. Mix the egg white, cornstarch, and salt in a medium bowl. Add the lobster and the vegetable oil. Mix well, cover, and refrigerate for 1 hour.

2. To begin the sauce, mix the stock, rice wine, salt, sugar, and white pepper in a small bowl. Dissolve the cornstarch in 1 tablespoon cold water in another small bowl. Set both bowls aside.

3. Bring a large, wide pot of water to a boil over high heat. Heat a large wok over high heat. Add enough oil to come about 1½ inches up the sides of the wok, and heat it to 300°F. Place a fine-mesh strainer over a heatproof bowl, and set it next to the stove. Turn off the heat under the water and under the wok. Beat the egg whites in a medium bowl until frothy. Pour some of the egg whites into the oil. They will puff up in a cloud in 5 seconds. Using a fine-mesh or slotted skimmer, remove them from the oil, dip them in the hot water, and transfer them to the strainer. Repeat until all the egg whites are cooked. Set aside.

4. Reheat the oil in the wok to 325°F. Add the lobster tails, one by one, and turn them constantly until they turn white, about 40 seconds, being careful not to let them brown. Using the skimmer, transfer the lobster tails to the cooked egg whites. Discard all but 2 tablespoons of the oil from the wok.

5. Return the wok with the oil to high heat. Add the sugar snap peas, bell pepper, scallions, and ginger, and stir-fry for 30 seconds. Return the lobster and egg whites to the wok, and add the tree ears and the stock mixture. Stir-fry until the lobster is evenly coated with the sauce, about 30 seconds. Add the cornstarch mixture and stir-fry for 10 seconds. Transfer to a platter, and serve.

ON A VISIT TO POSITANO, I ate a dish of spaghetti with langoustines, a small member of the lobster family, and had a minor epiphany. Why not create a Chinese version? This is the result. The soaked-until-softened bean threads can steam with the lobster for 7 minutes and still remain al dente. You will need a heatproof serving bowl that is large enough to hold the ingredients and fit into a steamer.

If you cannot find the bean thread vermicelli, substitute angel hair pasta, which should be cooked in boiling water for 30 seconds, then drained. The pasta will be quite firm, but remember that it will be steamed with the lobster to finish cooking. In most dishes featuring noodles, the Chinese traditionally do not cut them. Since noodles signify longevity, cutting them might bring bad luck.

Makes 2 to 4 servings

Steamed Lobster with Garlic over Bean Thread Vermicelli

4 ounces bean thread vermicelli (mung bean flour noodles)
$1/3$ cup olive oil
12 garlic cloves, peeled and minced
2 tablespoons soy sauce
$1/4$ cup rice wine or dry sherry
1 teaspoon sugar
One $1^1/_2$-pound lobster: 2 claws, the tail cut in half lengthwise, and the body chopped into 4 pieces (see Note)
$1^1/_2$ teaspoons ground white pepper

1. Heat 4 cups of water in a small saucepan over high heat until just steaming. Remove the pan from the heat and add the bean thread vermicelli. Soak until the vermicelli are softened, about 15 minutes.

2. Meanwhile, add 2 inches of water to the bottom of an Asian-style steamer, and bring it to a boil over high heat.

3. Heat the olive oil in a small skillet over medium-low heat until the it is hot and shimmering but not smoking. Add the garlic and cook until it is pale gold, about 2 minutes.

Steamed Lobster with Garlic over Bean Thread Vermicelli (continued)

Transfer the garlic and oil to a small bowl, and set it aside. Mix the soy sauce, rice wine, and sugar in another small bowl, and set it aside.

4. Drain the vermicelli well in a wire sieve. Place the noodles in a heatproof bowl with a cover that is large enough to hold the lobster pieces and will fit inside the steamer. Place the lobster on top of the vermicelli, and top with the garlic in olive oil. Sprinkle with the white pepper, and pour the soy sauce mixture over the top. Place the bowl in the steamer, cover, and steam over high heat until the lobster meat is white, 7 to 9 minutes. Serve immediately.

Note: Have the fishmonger cut up the lobster for you, and use it within a few hours of purchase.

THIS DISH OF HUGE CRISP SHRIMP with a dollop of sweetened mayonnaise and a toss of honeyed walnuts and emerald green broccoli arrived in North America in the early '80s. I wondered why the dish contained mayonnaise, which is not a Chinese ingredient. Apparently Chinese chefs in Hong Kong picked up mayonnaise from Western cooking and incorporated it into their cuisine.

Makes 4 servings

Grand Marnier Shrimp

12 colossal or jumbo shrimp (about 1¼ ounces each),
    peeled and deveined, with tail segment intact
¾ cup plus 1 teaspoon cornstarch
Pinch of salt

Sauce
½ cup mayonnaise
1½ tablespoons orange juice
1 tablespoon sugar
½ tablespoon sweetened condensed milk or heavy cream
1 teaspoon orange-flavored liqueur, preferably Grand Marnier

12 broccoli florets
Vegetable oil, for deep-frying
12 to 16 Honey-Glazed Walnuts (page 34)

1. Combine the shrimp, the 1 teaspoon cornstarch, and the pinch of salt in a medium bowl. Mix well, then rinse the shrimp under cold running water. Drain, and pat them dry with paper towels. Cut deeper into the deveining incision of each shrimp, taking care not to cut all the way through. Flatten them slightly under the flat side of a cleaver. Place the remaining ¾ cup cornstarch on a plate, and press each shrimp into the cornstarch, coating it thoroughly on both sides. Cover the shrimp, and refrigerate for 30 minutes (this allows them to absorb the cornstarch and be very crisp when fried).

2. To make the sauce, combine the mayonnaise, orange juice, sugar, sweetened condensed milk, and liqueur in a small bowl. Mix well. Set it aside.

3. Bring a medium saucepan of lightly salted water to a boil over high heat. Add the broccoli florets and cook until they turn bright green, about 1 minute. Drain and set aside.

4. Heat a large wok over high heat. Add enough oil to come about 1 inch up the sides of the wok, and heat it to 350°F. Add the shrimp to the oil, one at a time, taking care that they don't stick together. Deep-fry the shrimp, turning them occasionally, until they are golden and crisp, about 1½ minutes. Using a wide wire-mesh strainer, transfer them to paper towels to drain.

5. Arrange the shrimp on a platter, and garnish with the broccoli and honeyed walnuts. Spoon a tablespoon of the mayonnaise sauce over the wide half of each shrimp. Serve immediately.

KUNG PAO CHICKEN, perhaps the most popular of all Sichuan dishes, is all about balance. The sauce blends sweet, sour, and spicy, and the roasted peanuts add a crunchy contrast to the tender chicken—or in this case, shrimp. Once we saw the popularity of Kung Pao Chicken at Shun Lee, Chef T. T. Wang and I created this seafood variation on the theme.   **Makes 4 servings**

Kung Pao Shrimp

12 colossal or jumbo shrimp (about $1\frac{1}{4}$ ounces each),
   peeled and deveined
1 tablespoon plus 1 teaspoon cornstarch
Pinch of salt
$\frac{1}{2}$ large egg white (beat a whole white until foamy and
   measure out half)

Sauce

2 tablespoons soy sauce
2 tablespoons sugar
2 tablespoons rice wine or dry sherry
2 tablespoons distilled white vinegar
2 tablespoons Chicken Stock (page 70) or canned chicken broth
2 teaspoons hot bean paste
1 tablespoon cornstarch
Vegetable oil, for passing through
6 asparagus stalks, tough ends discarded, spears peeled and
   sliced diagonally into $\frac{1}{4}$-inch-thick pieces
8 dried hot red peppers
4 scallions, white part only, trimmed and sliced diagonally into $\frac{1}{4}$-inch pieces
2 garlic cloves, peeled and sliced $\frac{1}{8}$ inch thick
$\frac{1}{3}$ cup salted roasted peanuts

1. Combine the shrimp, the 1 teaspoon cornstarch, and the pinch of salt in a medium bowl. Mix well, then rinse the shrimp under cold running water. Drain, and pat them dry with paper towels. Cut deeper into the deveining incision of each shrimp, taking care not to cut all the way through. Flatten them slightly under the flat side of a cleaver. Return the shrimp to the bowl, add the egg white and the remaining 1 tablespoon cornstarch, and mix well.

2. To begin the sauce, mix the soy sauce, sugar, rice wine, vinegar, stock, and hot bean paste in a small bowl, and set it aside. Dissolve the cornstarch in 2 tablespoons cold water in another small bowl, and set it aside.

3. Heat a large wok over high heat. Add enough oil to reach about $1\frac{1}{2}$ inches up the sides of the wok, and heat it to 325°F. Add the shrimp, one at a time, taking care that they do not stick to each other. Stir gently until they turn white, about 40 seconds. Using a wide wire-mesh strainer, transfer the shrimp to a colander. Discard all but 3 tablespoons of the oil from the wok. Return the wok with the oil to high heat. Add the asparagus and cook until they turn bright green, about 30 seconds. Transfer the asparagus to a colander to drain.

4. Return the wok to high heat. Add the peppers, scallions, and garlic, and stir-fry for 30 seconds. Add the shrimp, asparagus, and soy sauce mixture. Add the cornstarch mixture and stir-fry until the sauce thickens, about 30 seconds. Add the peanuts and stir-fry for 10 seconds. Serve immediately.

LAKE TUNG TING, in Hunan province, is famous for its sweet, almost completely white, shrimp. Like Snow White Lobster Tail, this dish marries seafood with silken clouds of egg whites, but with subtle distinctions. The lobster simmers for a moment with the egg white, sugar snap peas, red bell peppers, and tree ears, while here the shrimp are stir-fried with a different array of vegetables—straw mushrooms, water chestnuts, and broccoli. Each component has its own flavor, color, and texture.

Makes 4 servings

Lake Tung Ting Shrimp

12 colossal or jumbo shrimp (about $1^1/_4$ ounces each), peeled and deveined
1 tablespoon plus 1 teaspoon cornstarch
Pinch of salt
1 large egg white
1 teaspoon vegetable oil

Sauce

2 tablespoons rice wine or dry sherry
$^1/_4$ cup Chicken Stock (page 70) or canned chicken broth
2 teaspoons cornstarch
1 teaspoon sugar
$^1/_4$ teaspoon salt
Pinch of ground white pepper

8 strands Chinese broccoli or 8 broccoli florets
Vegetable oil, for passing through
6 large egg whites
$^1/_2$ cup canned straw mushrooms, drained and rinsed
$^1/_2$ cup sliced water chestnuts
2 scallions, white part only, trimmed and sliced diagonally into $^1/_4$-inch pieces

1. Combine the shrimp, the 1 teaspoon cornstarch, and the pinch of salt in a medium bowl. Mix well, then rinse the shrimp under cold running water. Drain, and pat them dry with paper towels. Cut deeper into the deveining incision of each shrimp, taking care not to cut all the way through. Flatten them slightly under the flat side of a cleaver. Return the shrimp to the bowl, add the egg white, the remaining 1 tablespoon cornstarch, and the oil and mix well. Cover and refrigerate for 1 hour.

2. Meanwhile, to begin the sauce, mix the rice wine, stock, cornstarch, sugar, salt, and white pepper in a small bowl. Set it aside.

3. Bring a medium saucepan of water to a boil over high heat. Add the broccoli and cook until it turns bright green, about 1 minute. Drain in a colander and set aside.

4. Bring a large, wide pot of water to a boil over high heat. Heat a large wok over high heat. Add enough oil to come 1 inch up the sides of the wok, and heat it to 300°F. Place a fine-mesh strainer over a heatproof bowl, and set it next to the stove. Turn off the heat under the water and under the wok. Beat the egg whites in a medium bowl until frothy. Pour some of the egg whites into the oil. They will puff up in a cloud in 5 seconds. Using a fine-mesh or slotted skimmer, remove them from the oil, dip them in the hot water, and transfer them to the strainer. Repeat until all the egg whites are cooked. Set the egg whites aside.

5. Heat the oil in the wok to 325°F. Add the shrimp, one at a time, taking care that they do not stick to each other. Stir gently until they turn white, about 40 seconds. Using a wide wire-mesh strainer, transfer the shrimp to a colander. Discard all but 2 tablespoons of the oil from the wok.

6. Return the wok with the oil to high heat. Add the straw mushrooms, water chestnuts, and scallions, and stir-fry for 1 minute. Add the shrimp, egg whites, rice wine mixture, and broccoli, and stir-fry for 30 seconds. Serve immediately.

THE VIVID COLORS AND TASTES of this Sichuan dish make it a perennial favorite, with pink-white shrimp swaddled in a rich, spicy but not too hot red sauce and garnished with minced scallion greens. When cooked in its place of origin, it can be searingly hot, but we use less hot bean paste than is traditional, so all of the flavors share the spotlight. If you don't have the fermented rice, leave it out.

Makes 4 to 6 servings

Shrimp with Garlic and Scallions

1 pound colossal or jumbo shrimp (about 1$\frac{1}{4}$ ounces each),
    peeled and deveined
1 tablespoon plus 1 teaspoon cornstarch
Salt
1 large egg white
$\frac{1}{4}$ teaspoon ground white pepper
Vegetable oil, for passing through

Sauce
    $\frac{1}{3}$ cup rice wine or dry sherry
    2 tablespoons sugar
    2 tablespoons soy sauce
    $\frac{1}{4}$ teaspoon ground white pepper
    1$\frac{1}{2}$ tablespoons cornstarch

    $\frac{1}{4}$ onion, minced
    1$\frac{1}{2}$ scallions, trimmed, white and green parts separated and
        minced (about 2$\frac{1}{2}$ tablespoons each)
    1 tablespoon peeled and minced fresh ginger
    6 garlic cloves, peeled and minced
    1$\frac{1}{2}$ tablespoons hot bean paste
    2 tablespoons fermented rice, optional
    1 tablespoon dark sesame oil

1. Combine the shrimp, the 1 teaspoon cornstarch, and a pinch of salt in a medium bowl. Mix well, then rinse the shrimp under cold running water. Drain, and pat them dry with paper towels.

2. Mix the shrimp with the egg white, the remaining 1 tablespoon cornstarch, the white pepper, and $\frac{1}{8}$ teaspoon salt in a medium bowl.

3. Heat a large wok over high heat. Add enough oil to come 1 inch up the sides of the wok, and heat it to 325°F. Add the shrimp, one by one, taking care that they don't splash hot oil. Stir gently, turning the shrimp often, until they turn white, about 40 seconds. Using a wide wire-mesh strainer, transfer the shrimp to a colander to drain. Discard all but 2 tablespoons of the oil from the wok.

4. To begin the sauce, mix the rice wine, sugar, soy sauce, and white pepper in a small bowl, and set it aside. Dissolve the cornstarch in $\frac{1}{4}$ cup cold water in another small bowl, and set it aside.

5. Return the wok with the oil to high heat. Add the onion, white parts of the scallions, ginger, and garlic, and stir-fry until the onion becomes translucent, about 40 seconds. Add the hot bean paste, rice wine mixture, fermented rice if using, and $\frac{1}{3}$ cup water, and bring the mixture to a boil, about 30 seconds.

6. Return the shrimp to the wok. Add the cornstarch mixture, the green parts of the scallions, and the sesame oil, and stir-fry until the sauce thickens, about 20 seconds. Serve immediately.

WHILE WE PREFER JUMBO SHRIMP for many recipes, here it is best to use the smallest shrimp available, or even rock shrimp. Frozen baby peas are a better choice than the average-size large peas, but you have a choice here as well: shelled frozen soybeans (edamame) are also excellent.   **Makes 4 servings**

Sautéed Shrimp with Peas

1 pound small or medium shrimp, peeled and deveined
2 large egg whites
3 tablespoons cornstarch
$1/4$ teaspoon salt

Sauce
$1/2$ cup rice wine or dry sherry
1 tablespoon sugar
1 tablespoon red wine vinegar
$1/4$ teaspoon salt
2 tablespoons Chicken Stock (page 70) or canned chicken broth
1 teaspoon cornstarch

Vegetable oil, for passing through
4 scallions, white part only, trimmed and sliced diagonally into $1/2$-inch pieces
1 tablespoon peeled and minced fresh ginger
$3/4$ cup thawed frozen baby peas

1. Mix the shrimp, egg whites, cornstarch, and salt in a medium bowl. Cover and refrigerate for 45 minutes.

2. To begin the sauce, mix the rice wine, sugar, vinegar, and salt in a small bowl, and set it aside. Mix the stock, cornstarch, and 1 tablespoon cold water in another small bowl, and set it aside.

3. Heat a large wok over high heat. Add enough oil to come $1\frac{1}{2}$ inches up the sides of the wok, and heat it to 300°F. Quickly add the shrimp in 2 or 3 additions and stir gently until they turn white, about 1 minute. Using a wide wire-mesh strainer, transfer the shrimp to a colander to drain. Discard all but 2 tablespoons of the oil from the wok.

4. Return the wok with the oil to high heat. Add the scallions, ginger, and peas and stir-fry for 15 seconds Return the shrimp to the wok. Add the rice wine and cornstarch mixtures, and stir-fry until the sauce thickens, about 20 seconds. Serve immediately.

ONE OF THE EARLIEST SICHUAN DISHES introduced to the United States, this recipe combines spicy, sweet, and sour. It also includes tree ears, a black fungus that the Chinese believe will lower cholesterol. In Sichuan, the heat level is increased by using hot chili oil to cook the garlic and scallions, but our recipe provides plenty of spice without provoking tears. **Makes 4 servings**

Sichuan Shrimp

12 colossal or jumbo shrimp (about $1\frac{1}{4}$ ounces each), peeled and deveined
$\frac{3}{4}$ cup plus 1 teaspoon cornstarch
Salt

Sauce
$2\frac{1}{2}$ tablespoons sugar
2 tablespoons distilled white vinegar
2 tablespoons rice wine or dry sherry
2 tablespoons soy sauce
2 teaspoons hot bean paste
1 teaspoon cornstarch

Vegetable oil, for passing through
$\frac{1}{3}$ cup sliced canned bamboo shoots (cut before measuring into
    $\frac{1}{4}$-inch-thick strips about 2 inches long and 1 inch wide)
8 scallions, white part only, trimmed and sliced diagonally into $\frac{1}{4}$-inch pieces
10 dried red peppers
5 garlic cloves, peeled and sliced $\frac{1}{8}$ inch thick
$\frac{1}{4}$ cup tree ears, soaked in hot tap water until softened, drained and cut in half
1 teaspoon dark sesame oil

1. Combine the shrimp, the 1 teaspoon cornstarch, and a pinch of salt in a medium bowl. Mix well, and rinse the shrimp under cold running water. Drain, and pat them dry with paper towels. Mix the remaining $\frac{3}{4}$ cup cornstarch with a pinch of salt in a medium bowl. Dip the shrimp, one at a time, into the cornstarch, coating them thoroughly. Place the shrimp on a platter, cover with plastic wrap, and refrigerate for 30 minutes.

2. Meanwhile, to begin the sauce, mix the sugar, vinegar, rice wine, soy sauce, and hot bean paste in a small bowl. Dissolve the cornstarch in 2 tablespoons cold water in another small bowl. Set both bowls aside.

3. Heat a large wok over high heat. Add enough oil to come about 1 inch up the sides of the wok, and heat it to 325°F. Add the shrimp one at a time, taking care that they don't stick together, and stir gently until they turn white, about 40 seconds. Add the bamboo shoots in the last 10 seconds. Using a wide wire-mesh strainer, transfer the shrimp and bamboo shoots to a colander to drain. Discard all but 2 tablespoons of the oil from the wok.

4. Return the wok with the oil to high heat. Add the scallions, dried red peppers, and garlic, and stir-fry for 15 seconds. Return the shrimp and bamboo shoots to the wok, and then add the tree ears and the soy sauce mixture. Add the cornstarch mixture and stir-fry until the sauce thickens, about 20 seconds. Add the sesame oil at the last second. Serve immediately.

AT ONE PARTICULAR RESTAURANT in Shanghai, they serve 800 pounds of crab a day. Crab is never easy to eat from its shell, so this is a variation of an ancient Shanghai recipe, with sweet crabmeat out of the shell accented by a finish of black vinegar.

Makes 4 servings

Crabmeat with Snow Peas

4$\frac{1}{2}$ cups Chicken Stock (page 70), canned chicken broth, or water
8 ounces snow peas, trimmed, or pea shoots (see Note)
Vegetable oil, for passing through, plus 1 teaspoon
8 ounces fresh lump crabmeat, picked over for shells and cartilage
2 tablespoons rice wine or dry sherry
$\frac{1}{2}$ teaspoon salt
1 teaspoon sugar
1 teaspoon cornstarch
1 scallion, white part only, trimmed and minced
1 tablespoon peeled and minced fresh ginger
$\frac{1}{2}$ teaspoon dark sesame oil
4 teaspoons Chinese black or balsamic vinegar

1. Bring 4 cups of the stock to a boil in a medium saucepan. Add the snow peas and the 1 teaspoon vegetable oil, and cook until the snow peas turn bright green but still retain their crispness, about 15 seconds. Drain the snow peas in a colander; then transfer them to a serving platter. (If you are using pea shoots, wash the pea shoots and blanch them in the chicken stock until crisp-tender, about 1$\frac{1}{2}$ minutes. Drain the pea shoots in a colander, season them with a pinch of salt, and then transfer them to the serving platter.)

2. Heat a large wok over high heat. Add enough oil to come about 1$\frac{1}{2}$ inches up the sides of the wok, and heat it to 300°F. Add the crabmeat and cook for 30 seconds. Using a fine-mesh wire strainer, taking care that the crab doesn't fall through the slots, transfer the crab to a colander to drain. Discard all but 2 tablespoons of the oil from the wok.

3. Mix the remaining $\frac{1}{2}$ cup stock with the rice wine, salt, and sugar in a small bowl, and set it aside. Dissolve the cornstarch in 1 tablespoon cold water in another small bowl, and set it aside.

4. Return the wok with the oil to high heat. Add the scallion and ginger, and stir-fry for 15 seconds. Add the crabmeat and the stock mixture, and stir-fry until the crabmeat is hot, about 20 seconds. Stir in the cornstarch mixture and the sesame oil, and cook until the liquid thickens, about 10 seconds. Pour over the snow peas. Drizzle the black vinegar over the crabmeat and serve immediately.

Note: In China, this dish would be made with pea shoots, which can be found during the spring and early summer at Asian groceries and specialty markets.

Wine and Chinese Food

In China, a banquet always includes wine—usually copious amounts of warm Shaoxing rice wine. But at Shun Lee, I prefer to match dishes with the more familiar Western wines. For a large Chinese-style dinner with many individual courses, you may even serve moderate portions of different wines for each dish.

Begin with the traditional wine-and-food matching premise of serving white wines with light-flavored meats, poultry, and seafood, and red wines with red meat. But my wine advisor, Kenny Ng, suggests matching the wine to the strongest flavor in a dish. In many cases, these are spices and herbs. Here are a few of the most useful wines to inspire you to create your own matches of Chinese food and Western wines.

The floral and spicy notes of Gewürztraminer and Riesling are especially friendly matches with spicy chicken and seafood dishes, such as Curry Chicken with Hot and Sweet Peppers and Shrimp with Garlic and Scallions. Chardonnay can be paired with mildly flavored white meat dishes like Lion's Head with Cabbage and Sliced Chicken with Broccoli. Dishes with hot bean sauce, such as Sichuan Shrimp, call for the complex, honeyed qualities of Viognier.

When serving red meat, Pinot Noir goes well with lamb and duck dishes, as long as they aren't too spicy. The fruity-spicy notes in Zinfandel can mirror the same flavors in dishes like Sliced Duckling with Pickled Ginger. A full-bodied fruity, oaky Syrah will cut through the fat in rich dishes like Red-Cooked Beef Short ribs. Hunan Steak Kew, which in our version is made with filet mignon, will show how Cabernet Sauvignon retains its status as a time-honored partner of beef.

DUNGENESS CRAB, one of the glories of the Pacific coast, is now available all over the country, especially at Asian markets. Here is one of the best ways to cook it, with the cracked crab deep-fried, then topped with a wonderfully tasty mix of scallions, ginger, red onion, hot red pepper, coarsely ground black pepper, and a garnish of salty duck egg yolks. I give instructions for using either a cooked crab or a live one.

Makes 2 to 4 servings

Peppery Dungeness Crab

3 salty duck eggs

One 2-pound live Dungeness crab (for cooked crab, see Note)

$1/3$ cup cornstarch

Vegetable oil, for deep-frying

5 scallions, trimmed, white and green parts separated and minced

1 small red onion, peeled and minced

1 small fresh red chili, such as serrano, seeded and minced

1 teaspoon peeled and minced fresh ginger

6 garlic cloves, peeled and minced

1 tablespoon dark sesame oil

$3/4$ tablespoon coarsely ground black pepper, or to taste

2 tablespoons rice wine or dry sherry

Pinch of ground white pepper

1 teaspoon salt

1 teaspoon sugar

1. Preheat the oven to its lowest temperature, about 150°F. Bring a medium pot of water to a boil over high heat. Reduce the heat to medium, and slip in the duck eggs. Simmer for 8 minutes. Rinse the duck eggs under cold water. Shell them and discard the shells and the egg whites (unless you have a use for the egg whites, like serving them as a garnish for jook, the Chinese rice gruel). Mince the egg yolks. Spread the minced yolks on a baking sheet and bake until dried, about 30 minutes. Remove from the oven and let cool.

2. Bring a large pot of water to a rolling boil over high heat. Add the crab and cook until it stops moving, about 2 minutes. Drain, and rinse under cold water. Pull the legs off the crab and discard the feelers. Using a cleaver, chop off the tips of the claws and discard them. Turn the crab upside down. Using kitchen shears, carefully cut the

underside of the crab in half and remove it, leaving the carapace (top shell) intact. Scrape out and discard whatever is inside the carapace. Rinse the carapace and set it aside. Discard the gills and the material behind the head. Cut each half of the underside into 2 pieces. Using the blunt edge of the cleaver, crack the claws and legs so that the crab will absorb the flavors and be easy to open and eat.

3. Place the cornstarch in a medium bowl, and dip the crab pieces in it, tossing them until well coated. Heat a large wok over high heat. Add enough oil to come 2 inches up the sides of the wok, and heat it to 325°F. Fry the carapace until it turns deep red, about 30 seconds. Using a wide wire-mesh strainer, transfer it to a serving platter to use as decoration. In two or three batches, add the crab pieces to the wok, and stir gently for 4 minutes. Using the strainer, transfer the pieces to a colander to drain. Discard all but 2 tablespoons of the oil from the wok.

4. Return the wok with the oil to high heat, and add half the duck egg yolk, the white part of the scallions, and the red onion, chili, ginger, garlic, sesame oil, and black pepper. Stir-fry for 30 seconds. Return the crab to the wok and add the rice wine, white pepper, salt, and sugar. Stir-fry for 30 seconds, or until the crab is piping hot. Transfer to the platter with the carapace, and sprinkle with the green scallion tops and the remaining egg yolk. Serve immediately.

Note: If you have a cooked Dungeness crab, cut it up, following the instructions in step 2. Omit the cornstarch in step 3. Heat the oil as described, and fry the carapace for 30 seconds. Using a wide wire-mesh strainer, transfer it to a serving platter. Add the cooked crab pieces to the wok, and stir gently for 2 minutes. Using the strainer, transfer the pieces to a colander to drain. Discard all but 2 tablespoons of the oil from the wok. Continue with step 4.

THE CLASSIC FLAVORS of ginger and scallions are a perfect match to the sweetness of soft-shelled crabs. To provide the crabs with an extra measure of crispness, they are deep-fried for three short periods instead of one longer one.

Makes 2 to 4 servings

Soft-Shelled Crabs with Ginger and Scallions

2 soft-shelled crabs
$\frac{1}{4}$ cup all-purpose flour
Vegetable oil, for deep-frying, plus 2 tablespoons
1 scallion, white part only, trimmed and minced
1 tablespoon seeded and minced red bell pepper
1 tablespoon minced cilantro
1 teaspoon peeled and minced fresh ginger
1 tablespoon rice wine or dry sherry
Pinch of sugar
Pinch of salt
$\frac{1}{4}$ teaspoon dark sesame oil

1. To clean the crabs, lift up both sides of the shell and pull away and discard the gills and spongy (watery) part above the flesh. Do this on the bottom of the crab and the center (pointy) area as well. Also cut off the face of the crab, including the eyes.

2. Cut each crab into four pieces. Pour the flour into a bowl, and dip each piece of crab into the flour, shaking off any excess. Place the crab pieces on a plate.

3. Heat a large wok over high heat. Add enough oil to come $1\frac{1}{2}$ inches up the sides of the wok, and heat it to 375°F. Carefully add the crab pieces to the oil. Stand back—they will puff up and, because the crabs have a lot of water in them, they will sizzle and crackle. Deep-fry just until the coating is set, about 30 seconds. Using a wide wire-mesh strainer, transfer them to a colander.

4. Reheat the oil to 375°F. Return the crabs to the oil and deep-fry for 30 seconds more. Transfer to the colander. Reheat the oil again to 375°F. Return the crabs to the

oil and deep-fry until the sizzle in the oil slows down and the crabs are very crisp, about 30 seconds more. Transfer the crabs to the colander. Discard the oil and wipe out the wok with paper towels.

5. Return the wok to high heat. Add the 2 tablespoons oil and heat it. Add the scallion, bell pepper, cilantro, and ginger, and stir-fry for 30 seconds. Return the crab pieces to the wok and add the rice wine, sugar, salt, and sesame oil. Stir-fry for 30 seconds. Serve immediately.

I HAVE INTRODUCED AMERICAN DINERS to many new dishes, but the favor has been returned many times over. I never had soft-shelled crabs in China, and the first time I ate them at Manhattan's Le Cirque, I immediately went into my kitchen to create this dish. Tempura batter makes the coating very light and crisp, and in order to retain this texture, the crabs are topped, but not swathed, in the piquant black bean sauce. If you wish, you can serve the sauce on the side. Steamed asparagus would be a fine side dish. **Makes 2 to 4 servings**

Soft-Shelled Crabs with Black Bean Sauce

2 soft-shelled crabs
$1/3$ cup tempura batter mix (see Note)
1 large egg white, beaten until foamy

Sauce

$1/2$ cup Chicken Stock (page 70) or canned chicken broth
1 tablespoon soy sauce
1 tablespoon rice wine or dry sherry
2 teaspoons sugar
$1/4$ teaspoon ground white pepper
1 teaspoon cornstarch

Vegetable oil, for deep-frying, plus 2 tablespoons
2 scallions, white part only, trimmed and minced
$1/4$ cup minced canned bamboo shoots
2 garlic cloves, peeled and minced
1 teaspoon peeled and minced fresh ginger
1 tablespoon Chinese fermented black beans, mashed and minced
1 large egg, beaten

1. To clean the crabs, lift up both sides of the shell and pull away and discard the gills and the spongy (watery) part above the flesh. Do this on the bottom of the crab and the center (pointy) area as well. Also cut off the face of the crab, including the eyes.

2. Combine the tempura mix, egg white, and 1½ tablespoons water in a small bowl, stirring until it has the consistency of heavy cream. If necessary, add a bit more water to get the right consistency.

3. To begin the sauce, mix the stock, soy sauce, rice wine, sugar, and white pepper in a small bowl, and set it aside. Dissolve the cornstarch in 2 teaspoons cold water in another small bowl, and set it aside.

4. Heat a large wok over high heat. Add enough oil to come about 1½ inches up the sides of the wok, and heat it to 375°F. Dip the crabs, one at a time, into the tempura batter to coat them, letting the excess batter drip back into the bowl. Carefully add the crabs to the oil. Stand back—they will puff up, and because the crabs have a lot of water in them, the oil will sizzle and crackle. Deep-fry until the crabs are crisp and golden, about 3 minutes. One way to check for doneness is to listen to the sizzle: When it is quite slow, but before it disappears, use a wide wire-mesh strainer to transfer the crabs to a colander to drain. Cut each crab into four pieces and place them on a serving platter. Discard the oil, and wipe the wok clean with paper towels.

5. Return the wok to medium-high heat and add the 2 tablespoons oil. Add the scallions, bamboo shoots, garlic, ginger, and black beans, and stir-fry for 30 seconds. Add the chicken stock mixture and stir for 30 seconds. Stir in the cornstarch mixture. Using a circular motion, pour the beaten egg slowly into the bean sauce so it floats on top of the sauce, and cook until the egg sets.

6. Spoon the sauce over the crabs, or serve it on the side. Serve immediately.

Note: Tempura batter mix is a commercial blend of flour, cornstarch, leavenings, and dried eggs that makes an especially light coating for deep-fried foods. It is available at Asian and Japanese groceries and in many supermarkets.

Poultry

CHICKEN AND DUCK are treated with the deepest respect by Chinese cooks because they represent the mythological phoenix, the monster with the head of a pheasant and the tail of a peacock that destroys itself in flames, only to be reborn again. The phoenix, and therefore all poultry, is associated with immortality. Chinese mythology states that wherever the phoenix rests, there will be a golden egg laid underneath, and therefore the phoenix also represents prosperity.

In the past two decades, chicken has become so popular that it is replacing pork as the most popular meat in China. Tasty, satisfying, and extremely versatile, it is the main ingredient in some of the most distinctive and flavorful dishes in Chinese cuisine. Beyond the familiar techniques of stir-frying and deep-frying, which are used for two of the most famous of all Chinese chicken dishes, Chengdu Chicken and Kung Pao Chicken, you will also find chicken baked under a thick layer of salt and chicken simmered with soy sauce and spices. No matter which recipe you choose, the result will be juicy and tender, as befits an "immortal" bird.

Duck is usually reserved for very festive occasions celebrated at restaurants. Nonetheless, it is worthwhile to make duck dishes at home because the results are so rewarding. The duck recipes here run the gamut from homey to sophisticated.

CRISPY DEEP-FRIED CHUNKS of chicken thighs are melded with a unique sauce that combines sugar, vinegar, and chilies. You might recognize this as General Tso's Chicken, which is found on almost every Chinese menu today. Chef Wang and I introduced it to this country at Hunam Restaurant over thirty years ago. At Shun Lee we leave out the handfuls of dried chili peppers that other restaurants insist on using in their versions, and we call it Chengdu Chicken, after the capital city of Sichuan.

Makes 4 servings

Chengdu Chicken

1 pound boneless, skinless chicken thighs, cut into 1-inch cubes
1 large egg
$1/4$ cup cornstarch
$1/2$ teaspoon salt
Vegetable oil, for deep-frying

Sauce
$1/4$ cup minced sweet American pickles (sweet gherkins)
3 tablespoons distilled white vinegar
3 tablespoons sugar
2 tablespoons soy sauce
2 tablespoons rice wine or dry sherry
1 tablespoon Vietnamese or Thai fish sauce
2 teaspoons hot bean paste
1 teaspoon cornstarch
1 scallion, white and green parts, trimmed and minced
2 garlic cloves, peeled and sliced $1/8$ inch thick
1 small hot chili pepper, such as Thai or cayenne, seeded and minced
6 cilantro sprigs, for garnish

1. Mix the chicken, egg, cornstarch, salt, and 1 tablespoon water in a medium bowl. Cover and refrigerate for 30 minutes.

2. Heat a large wok over high heat. Add enough oil to come about $1^{1}/2$ inches up the sides of the wok, and heat it to 375°F. In two batches, add the chicken pieces to the oil, a few pieces at a time (so they don't splash or stick together), and stir gently, keeping the pieces separate and cooking until the coating looks set but not browned, about

45 seconds. Using a wide wire-mesh skimmer, transfer the chicken to a colander to drain. Using a fine-mesh strainer or skimmer, remove any bits of fried chicken or batter from the oil. Reheat the oil to 375°F. Return the chicken to the wok, and deep-fry again until it is golden brown and crispy, about 2 minutes. Transfer to paper towels to drain. Discard all but 2 tablespoons of the oil from the wok.

3. To begin the sauce, mix the pickles, vinegar, sugar, soy sauce, rice wine, fish sauce, and hot bean paste in a small bowl. Dissolve the cornstarch in 1 tablespoon cold water in another small bowl. Set the bowls aside.

4. Return the wok with the oil to high heat. Add the scallion, garlic, and chili, and stir-fry until the scallion wilts, about 15 seconds. Return the chicken to the wok and add the pickle mixture. Stir-fry for 20 seconds. Add the cornstarch mixture and stir-fry until the sauce thickens, about 10 seconds. Garnish the chicken with the cilantro, and serve immediately.

CURRY SHOWS UP in a few Chinese dishes. Here, a spectacular sauce with layered flavors of curry, coconut milk, and red pepper (sweet and hot) shows off the versatility of chicken. It is good the second, and even the third day. You can substitute shrimp for the chicken, or for a vegetarian curry, substitute cooked potatoes, cauliflower, and green beans for the chicken. If you want to make the curry a day ahead, cook and add the okra just before serving.   **Makes 4 to 6 servings**

Curry Chicken with Hot and Sweet Peppers

24 okra pods
One 3$\frac{1}{2}$-pound chicken

Sauce

$\frac{1}{2}$ large red bell pepper, seeds and ribs discarded, minced
2 tablespoons hot chili oil
$\frac{1}{4}$ cup vegetable oil
$\frac{1}{3}$ cup peeled and minced red onion
$\frac{1}{3}$ cup peeled and minced white onion
3 tablespoons peeled and minced garlic
1$\frac{1}{2}$ tablespoons minced lemongrass (use the peeled, tender bulb end only)
1$\frac{1}{2}$ tablespoons peeled and minced galangal
1 tablespoon peeled and minced fresh ginger
3 Keffir lime leaves, optional
$\frac{1}{4}$ cup curry powder
2 cups Chicken Stock (page 70) or canned chicken broth
$\frac{1}{4}$ cup ketchup
1 tablespoon sugar
2 whole star anise
1 teaspoon salt
One 13.5-ounce can of coconut milk (regular or light)

1. Trim the stem ends and tips from the okra. Place the okra in a medium bowl and add cold water to cover. Set aside.

2. Bring a large pot of water to a boil over high heat. Using a cleaver, cut the wings, thighs, and drumsticks from the chicken. Chop off and discard the wing tips; then chop

the wings in half through the joint. Chop each thigh and drumstick in half. Chop the carcass in half lengthwise, then chop it into 16 pieces, each about $1\frac{1}{2}$ by 2 inches. Add the chicken to the water and return the water to a boil. Remove from the heat, cover, and let stand for 10 minutes while you prepare the sauce. This will cook the chicken by about 40 percent.

3. To begin the sauce, mix the red bell pepper with the hot chili oil in a small bowl to combine. Set it aside.

4. Heat a large wok over high heat. Add the vegetable oil and heat until it is shimmering but not smoking. Add the red and white onions, garlic, lemongrass, galangal, ginger, and optional lime leaves, and stir-fry until the onions soften around the edges, about 30 seconds. Add the red pepper mixture and stir continuously over medium-high heat until the sauce turns red, about 7 minutes. It should simmer and gently bubble. If you have to stop to attend to something else, turn off the heat.

5. Meanwhile, bring a medium saucepan of water to a boil over high heat. Drain the okra and add it to the saucepan. Cook until tender, about 5 minutes. Drain.

6. Return to the sauce, and if you had turned off the heat, bring the sauce back to a simmer. Add the curry powder, then the stock, ketchup, sugar, star anise, and salt, and stir for 30 seconds. Drain the chicken and add it to the wok. Stir in the coconut milk and bring the sauce to a simmer. Cook until the chicken shows no pink when it is pierced at the bone, 10 minutes. During the last minute, add the okra. Remove the star anise and lime leaves, if using, and serve immediately.

IN SICHUAN, during the mid-nineteenth century Qing Dynasty, there was a governor and court official named Ting, who was a famous gourmet. One story goes that the governor's chef was cooking this dish and accidentally burned the red chilies. His guests, perhaps out of politeness, all remarked on how delicious it was. In Mandarin, *kung pao* means "court official," so the dish came to be known as kung pao chicken. If anyone at your table is allergic to peanuts, eliminate them.

Makes 4 servings

Kung Pao Chicken

12 ounces boneless, skinless chicken breast, cut into $3/4$-inch cubes
1 large egg white, beaten until foamy
1 teaspoon cornstarch
1 teaspoon salt

Sauce
$1/4$ cup rice wine or dry sherry
2 tablespoons soy sauce
2 tablespoons red wine vinegar
2 tablespoons sugar
1 teaspoon cornstarch

Vegetable oil, for passing through, plus 2 tablespoons
6 scallions, white and green parts, trimmed and sliced into $1/4$-inch pieces (1 cup)
2 garlic cloves, peeled and sliced $1/8$ inch thick
10 small dried hot red chilies
$1\frac{1}{2}$ teaspoons hot bean sauce
$1/2$ cup salted roasted peanuts
1 teaspoon dark sesame oil

1. Mix the chicken, egg white, cornstarch, and salt in a bowl. Cover and refrigerate for 30 minutes.

2. To begin the sauce, mix the rice wine, soy sauce, vinegar, and sugar in a small bowl, and set it aside. Dissolve the cornstarch in 2 tablespoons cold water in another small bowl, and set it aside.

3. Heat a large wok over high heat. Add enough vegetable oil to come about 1½ inches up the sides of the wok, and heat it to 325°F. Add the chicken pieces, one at a time so the pieces don't splash or stick to each other, and stir gently, keeping the pieces of chicken separate and cooking until they turn white, about 45 seconds. Using a wide wire-mesh strainer, transfer the chicken to a colander to drain. Discard the oil from the wok. Wipe out the wok with paper towels.

4. Place the wok over medium-high heat. Add the 2 tablespoons vegetable oil and heat until it is shimmering. Add the scallions, garlic, chilies, and hot bean sauce, and stir-fry until the scallions wilt, about 30 seconds. Return the chicken to the wok, add the rice wine mixture, and stir-fry until the chicken is heated through, about 30 seconds. Add the cornstarch mixture and stir until the sauce thickens, a few seconds more. Add the peanuts and sesame oil, and mix well. Serve immediately.

THE ORIGINAL LEMON CHICKEN, developed by Cantonese chefs, was pan-fried chicken in a tangy-sweet lemon sauce. Sometime in the '50s, the chicken started being deep-fried and promptly became an American sensation, and even a dinner party favorite. At its best, when made with fresh lemons and water chestnut flour (readily available in Asian markets), the batter ensures an especially crisp crust. This is fried chicken with a difference. Whenever I try to remove Lemon Chicken from the menu, people beg me to reinstate it.

You can substitute regular all-purpose flour for the water chestnut flour, but the crust will not be as thoroughly crisp. **Makes 4 to 6 servings**

Lemon Chicken

Sauce
2 lemons
Two ½-inch-thick slices peeled fresh ginger, smashed under a cleaver
1 cup sugar
1 tablespoon cornstarch

Three 5- to 6-ounce boneless, skinless chicken breasts,
    each cut horizontally to make thin cutlets
2 tablespoons all-purpose flour
1 large egg
1 teaspoon soy sauce
½ teaspoon rice wine or dry sherry
¼ teaspoon salt
¼ teaspoon ground white pepper
¾ cup water chestnut flour
Vegetable oil, for deep-frying

1. To make the sauce, remove the yellow zest from the lemons in long strips, using a vegetable peeler. Cut the strips into very thin shreds and set them aside for the garnish. Cut off the white pith from the lemons, and cut each lemon crosswise into 8 rounds.

2. Bring 1 cup water to a boil in a small saucepan. Add the lemon slices and ginger, and cook for 4 minutes. Remove from the heat. Discard the ginger, and strain the

liquid into a bowl, pressing down on the lemon slices to extract the juice. Pour the strained lemon liquid back into the pan and stir in the sugar. Bring to a boil over medium-high heat, stirring to dissolve the sugar. Dissolve the cornstarch in 1 tablespoon cold water in a small bowl, and stir into the sauce. Remove from the heat and partially cover to keep the sauce warm.

3. Using the flat side of a cleaver or a flat meat mallet, pound the chicken on both sides to $1/4$- to $1/2$-inch thickness. Mix the flour, egg, soy sauce, rice wine, salt, and white pepper in a medium bowl until smooth. Fill one shallow dish with $1/2$ cup water, and another shallow dish with the water chestnut flour. Dip each slice of chicken first into the batter so it is completely coated, then into the water, and then into the water chestnut flour, pressing the flour firmly into the chicken so it adheres.

4. Heat a large wok over high heat. Add enough oil to come about 2 inches up the sides of the wok, and heat it to 375°F. Working in two batches without crowding, add the chicken, one piece at a time, to the oil. The pieces should float in the oil, and bubbles will immediately form around them. Deep-fry, turning once, just until the chicken is pale gold, about $2\frac{1}{2}$ minutes. Using a wide wire-mesh strainer, transfer the chicken to a colander to drain. Reheat the oil to 375°F. Return the chicken to the oil and deep-fry again until golden brown and cooked through, about $1\frac{1}{2}$ minutes, depending on the thickness of the meat. Transfer to paper towels to drain. Discard the oil.

5. On a chopping board, cut the chicken crosswise into 12 to 16 pieces, and place them on a serving platter. Pour the sauce over the chicken, and garnish with the lemon zest. Serve immediately.

THIS POPULAR HOME-STYLE Eastern China dish is the perfect meal for a cold winter night. Rock sugar, which has a honey-like richness, enhances the inherent sweetness of the chestnuts, and the warm spices in the sauce—the cinnamon, star anise, ginger, and peppers—will fill your kitchen with the irresistible aromas of a red-cooked dish. Vacuum-packed cooked chestnuts are available at Asian markets and many supermarkets.

Traditionally, when the Chinese make a red-cooked chicken, they cut a four-pound chicken into 12 to 14 pieces, with the bone and the skin on. The chicken will take 45 minutes to cook. But because Shun Lee doesn't usually like to serve chicken on the bone to its customers, we have simplified the dish and cook the boneless chicken in much less time. **Makes 4 servings**

Red-Cooked Chicken with Chestnuts

Vegetable oil, for passing through
14 ounces boneless, skinless chicken thighs, pounded to $1/2$-inch thickness
    and cut into 1-inch pieces
1 cup (6 ounces) peeled cooked chestnuts
1 scallion, trimmed and cut in half
One $1/2$-inch-thick slice peeled fresh ginger, smashed under a cleaver
$1 1/2$ tablespoons smashed rock sugar
$1/2$ cinnamon stick, about 2 inches long
4 dried hot red peppers
1 whole star anise
3 tablespoons rice wine or dry sherry
$1/4$ cup soy sauce
1 cup Chicken Stock (page 70) or canned chicken broth
1 tablespoon cornstarch
1 teaspoon dark sesame oil

1. Heat a large wok over high heat. Add enough vegetable oil to come $1 1/2$ inches up the sides of the wok, and heat it to 300°F. Add the chicken pieces, one at a time so they don't splash or stick to each other, and stir gently until they turn white, about 1 minute. Add the chestnuts and fry for 20 seconds. Using a wide wire-mesh strainer, transfer the chicken and chestnuts to a colander to drain. Discard all but 2 tablespoons of the oil from the wok.

2. Return the wok with the oil to medium-high heat. Add the scallion, ginger, rock sugar, cinnamon, dried peppers, and star anise, and cook, reducing the heat as needed so the scallion doesn't burn. Return the chicken and chestnuts to the wok, add the rice wine and soy sauce, and cook for 30 seconds. Add the stock and bring to a boil over high heat. Continue cooking, stirring often, until the sauce is reduced to a glossy syrup, about 5 minutes. Using a slotted spoon, remove and discard the peppers, cinnamon, star anise, scallion, and ginger.

3. Dissolve the cornstarch in 3 tablespoons cold water in a small bowl, and stir into the wok. Add the sesame oil and simmer for 20 seconds. Serve immediately.

SURROUNDED WITH FRAGRANT SALT and cooked on top of the stove, this chicken is truly succulent. (This preparation is vaguely related to clay-wrapped and baked Beggar's Chicken, which is served at Shun Lee but is a bit daunting for the home cook.) The salt seals in flavor and juiciness. Be sure that your wok has a lid.

Makes 4 to 6 servings

Salt-Crusted Chicken

5 pounds plus 2 tablespoons fine sea salt (see Note)
1 lemongrass stalk, tender bulb part only, trimmed, peeled,
    and cut into 2-inch-long pieces
One 3-inch cinnamon stick, broken into 4 pieces
5 whole star anise
20 Sichuan peppercorns
1 scallion, white part only, trimmed and minced
1 tablespoon rice wine or dry sherry
2 teaspoons ground ginger
1 teaspoon five-spice powder
One 4-pound chicken
1 tablespoon vegetable oil
1 piece parchment paper, large enough to wrap the chicken

1. Preheat the oven to 450°F. Mix the 5 pounds of sea salt with the lemongrass, cinnamon stick, star anise, and Sichuan peppercorns in an ovenproof casserole or roasting pan. Place the pan in the oven and bake until the spices give off their aromas, about 20 minutes. Turn off the oven, and set aside.

2. Bring a large saucepan of water to a boil over high heat. Mix the 2 tablespoons sea salt, scallion, rice wine, ground ginger, and five-spice powder in a small bowl. Rub the mixture into the inside of the chicken cavity. Add the chicken to the water and cook for 15 seconds to tighten the skin and make it shiny. (Remarkably, the spices in the chicken cavity will not come out.) Drain the chicken in a colander.

3. Rub the oil all over the chicken, and wrap the chicken in the parchment paper. Pour one third of the salt mixture into a large wok. Place the wrapped chicken on top, and pour the rest of the salt mixture over the chicken, covering it completely. Cover the wok, and cook over medium-high or high heat for 1 hour. You should see a tiny wisp

of smoke occasionally rising from the wok. If you don't see a wisp of smoke, turn up the heat slightly until there is a bit of smoke. After 1 hour, remove the chicken, unwrap it, and cut into a thigh to make sure it's cooked. If it's still slightly pink, rewrap the chicken, return it to the wok, bury it in the salt, and cook for another 10 minutes or until the thigh is no longer pink.

4. Remove and unwrap the hot chicken. Slice off the legs and the wings. Chop the chicken in half lengthwise, then chop each half into 8 pieces. Serve immediately.

Note: Sea salt is available in bulk at natural food stores and some supermarkets.

THIS LIGHT BUT FLAVORFUL DISH features silken slices of chicken breast tossed with crunchy broccoli. Usually the chicken is passed through the oil, but there are alternatives. If you wish, after blanching the vegetables, cook the chicken in the stock until it turns white, about 1 minute, then drain. Or skip the passing through altogether, and stir-fry the chicken in 1 tablespoon of vegetable oil before adding the garlic and scallions. For a spicier dish, add some crushed hot red pepper flakes.

To slice meat that is $1/8$ inch thick or even thinner, pound the meat with the flat side of a cleaver, and then slice it on a shallow diagonal across the grain.

Makes 4 servings

Sliced Chicken with Broccoli

2 boneless, skinless chicken breasts (10 ounces total)
1 large egg white
2 tablespoons cornstarch
$3/4$ teaspoon salt
4 cups plus $1/3$ cup Chicken Stock (page 70), canned chicken broth, or water
10 ounces broccoli florets
$1/2$ cup sliced water chestnuts ($1/4$-inch-thick slices)
12 canned straw mushrooms, rinsed and drained
1 teaspoon sugar
2 tablespoons rice wine or dry sherry
Vegetable oil, for passing through
2 scallions, white part only, trimmed and minced
3 garlic cloves, peeled and minced

1. Slice chicken breasts in half horizontally. Flatten the chicken breasts by pounding them on both sides with the flat side of a cleaver or a flat meat mallet until $1/8$ inch thick. Slice the meat on a shallow diagonal to make 1-inch-wide strips. Cut the strips into $1^1/2$-inch pieces.

2. Mix the chicken, egg white, 1 tablespoon of the cornstarch, and $1/4$ teaspoon of the salt in a medium bowl. Set it aside.

3. Bring the 4 cups chicken stock to a boil in a medium saucepan over high heat. Add the broccoli, water chestnuts, and straw mushrooms, and cook until the broccoli

is crisp-tender, about 1½ minutes. Transfer the vegetables to a strainer to drain, and discard the broth.

4. Mix the remaining ⅓ cup chicken stock with the remaining ½ teaspoon salt, the sugar and the rice wine in a small bowl. Dissolve the remaining 1 tablespoon cornstarch in 3 tablespoons cold water in a small bowl. Set the bowls aside.

5. Heat a large wok over high heat. Add enough oil to come about 1 inch up the sides of the wok, and heat it to 300°F. Add the chicken pieces, a few at a time, and stir gently, so the pieces don't stick to each other, until the chicken turns white, about 1 minute. Using a wide wire-mesh strainer, transfer the chicken to a colander to drain. Discard all but 2 tablespoons of the oil from the wok.

6. Return the wok with the oil to high heat. Add the scallions and garlic, and stir-fry until the garlic is fragrant, about 10 seconds. Add the stock mixture and the cornstarch mixture, and bring to a boil. Return the chicken and vegetables to the wok, and stir-fry until the sauce has thickened, about 30 seconds. Serve immediately.

SHUN LEE INVENTED THIS Sichuan-style dish in 1965, serving tender shreds of chicken in a spicy sauce on a bed of spinach.   **Makes 4 servings**

Slippery Chicken

10 ounces boneless, skinless chicken breast, cut into 1½-inch-long julienne
1 large egg white
1 tablespoon cornstarch
¼ teaspoon salt
Vegetable oil, for passing through

Spinach

5 cups Chicken Stock (page 70), canned chicken broth, or water
One 10-ounce bag tender leaf spinach, well rinsed

Sauce

3 tablespoons Chicken Stock (page 70) or canned chicken broth
2 tablespoons rice wine or dry sherry
2 tablespoons soy sauce
2 tablespoons distilled white vinegar
2 tablespoons sugar
Pinch of ground white pepper
1 tablespoon cornstarch

2 scallions, white and green parts, trimmed and minced
4 garlic cloves, peeled and minced
2 teaspoons peeled and minced fresh ginger
2 teaspoons hot bean paste
1 teaspoon hot chili oil

1. Mix the chicken, egg white, cornstarch, salt, and 1 tablespoon of the vegetable oil in a medium bowl. Set it aside.

2. To prepare the spinach, bring the stock to a boil in a medium saucepan over high heat. Add 1 tablespoon of the vegetable oil, then the spinach, and cook until the spinach turns bright green, about 45 seconds. Drain thoroughly in a colander. Spread the spinach on a serving platter and cover with aluminum foil to keep warm.

3. Heat a large wok over high heat. Add enough vegetable oil to come 1 inch up the sides of the wok, and heat it to 300°F. Add the chicken pieces, a few at a time, in small batches and stir gently, keeping the pieces separate and cooking until the chicken turns white, about 45 seconds. Using a wide-mesh strainer, transfer the chicken to a colander to drain. Discard all but 2 tablespoons of the oil from the wok.

4. To begin the sauce, mix the 3 tablespoons stock, rice wine, soy sauce, vinegar, sugar, and white pepper in a small bowl. Dissolve the cornstarch in $1/3$ cup cold water in another small bowl. Set the bowls aside.

5. Return the wok with the oil to high heat and add the scallions, garlic, and ginger. Stir-fry until the garliic is fragrant, about 10 seconds. Add the chicken stock mixture, hot bean paste, and the cornstarch mixture, and bring to a boil, about 10 seconds. Return the chicken to the wok, add the hot chili oil, and stir-fry until the chicken is cooked through, about 30 seconds. Pour on top of the spinach and serve immediately.

THIS RED-COOKED SHANGHAINESE DUCK is especially appropriate for winter. It is easy to make, and when served with steamed rice, it is a one-dish meal, combining duck with baby bok choy, mushrooms, carrots, and bamboo shoots. Like all the classic red-cooked dishes, its aroma is redolent of cinnamon and star anise. And when making a Chinese-style dinner party with many courses, this is a perfect choice because it can be made 24 hours in advance. If you do make it ahead of time, stop cooking at the end of step 3. Cool, cover, and refrigerate the duck in the sauce. The next day, about 30 minutes before you are going to serve the duck, continue with step 4 to reduce the sauce, cook the vegetables, and finish the dish.

Makes 4 to 6 servings

Braised Duck with Vegetables

One 6-pound duck
Vegetable oil, for passing through
$1/2$ cup soy sauce, plus more as needed
1 whole star anise
One 3-inch cinnamon stick
6 cups Chicken Stock (page 70) or canned chicken broth
1 cup rice wine or dry sherry
$1/2$ cup sugar
3 scallions, trimmed and cut in half
Three $1/8$-inch-thick slices peeled fresh ginger
3 small dried hot red chilies
1 teaspoon ground white pepper
10 Chinese dried black mushrooms, soaked in hot tap water until softened,
    drained and stems trimmed
16 baby bok choy or bok choy hearts
2 medium carrots, peeled and cut into wedges $1^1/2$ inches long and $1/2$ inch thick
$3/4$ cup sliced canned bamboo shoots, cut before measuring into slices $1^1/2$ inches long
    and $1/2$ inch thick, drained and rinsed
1 tablespoon cornstarch, optional

1. To prepare the duck, discard the neck, gizzard, and extra fat. Using a cleaver, chop the duck in half lengthwise. Cut off the wings. Cut off the drumstick and thigh portions at the hip joints. Chop each half of the duck body into 3 pieces. You will have

10 pieces of duck. Rinse the duck under cold running water, and pat it dry with paper towels.

2. Heat a heavy-bottomed casserole or Dutch oven over high heat. Add enough oil to come about 2 inches up the sides of the pot, and heat it to 350°F. Place the ½ cup soy sauce in a bowl, and dip each piece of duck in it (the soy sauce adds both color and flavor). Set the duck pieces aside, and add enough extra soy sauce to the bowl to bring it back to ½ cup. Set the soy sauce aside. In batches without crowding, add the duck pieces to the pot, and cook until the skin turns golden, about 2½ minutes. Using a wide wire-mesh strainer, transfer the duck to a colander to drain. Discard the oil.

3. Return the pot to high heat. Place the duck wings, star anise, and cinnamon stick on the bottom of the pot. (They will act as a rack for the rest of the duck and keep it from sticking to the bottom.) Add the rest of the duck, the ½ cup soy sauce, and the stock, rice wine, sugar, scallions, ginger, dried chilies, and white pepper. Place the mushrooms on top, and bring the liquid to a boil. Cover the pot, and reduce the heat to medium-low, so the broth bubbles gently. Cook for 1 hour, until the duck is quite tender but not falling off the bone.

4. Uncover the pot, turn the heat to high, and boil to reduce the sauce by two thirds, until it becomes glossy and syrupy, about 20 minutes. If the sauce has not reduced enough after 20 minutes, transfer the duck and mushrooms to a plate and set it aside, covered with aluminum foil to keep warm; continue reducing the sauce until syrupy and glossy. Using a slotted spoon, remove the scallions, ginger, star anise, cinnamon stick, and chilies, and discard.

5. While the sauce is reducing, prepare the vegetables: Bring a large saucepan of lightly salted water to a boil over high heat. Add the bok choy and cook until crisp-tender, about 1½ minutes. Using a mesh strainer, transfer the bok choy to a colander to drain. Arrange the bok choy on a serving platter, placing the leafy tops in the center. Add the carrots to the saucepan and cook until crisp-tender, about 1½ minutes. During the last 10 seconds, add the bamboo shoots. Using the mesh strainer, transfer the carrots and bamboo shoots to a colander to drain. Add the carrots and bamboo shoots to the pot. If the sauce is still too thin, dissolve cornstarch in 3 tablespoons cold water in a small bowl, stir into the pot, and cook just until the sauce thickens.

6. Using a slotted spoon, place the duck and mushrooms in the center of the bok choy. Spoon the sauce and vegetables over the duck. Serve immediately.

IN THE SPRING, young fresh ginger makes its annual appearance in Chinese markets. It is often paired with duck, where its tang cuts through the richness of the duck meat. These roots (well, actually rhizomes) have thin, pale yellow skin, pink tips, and a milder flavor than the older ginger we use the rest of the year. But they are seasonal and hard to find. To make this dish year-round, substitute Chinese pickled ginger, which has a tender texture and mild flavor similar to young ginger, and is not unlike the Japanese ginger served with sushi.

Makes 4 servings

Sliced Duckling with Pickled Ginger

1 boneless duck breast (available at specialty markets)
1 large egg white
1 teaspoon cornstarch
1 teaspoon salt
Vegetable oil, for passing through
$^{1}/_{4}$ cup sliced water chestnuts ($^{1}/_{8}$-inch-thick slices)

Sauce

2 tablespoons soy sauce
2 tablespoons sugar
2 tablespoons rice wine or dry sherry
1 tablespoon distilled white vinegar
1 tablespoon Chicken Stock (page 70) or canned chicken broth
1 teaspoon cornstarch

8 scallions, white and green parts, trimmed and sliced
    diagonally into $^{1}/_{2}$-inch pieces
3 garlic cloves, peeled and sliced $^{1}/_{8}$ inch thick
2 teaspoons hot bean paste
$^{1}/_{3}$ cup sliced bottled pickled ginger (cut $1^{1}/_{2}$ inches long,
    1 inch wide, and $^{1}/_{8}$ inch thick)
3 Chinese dried black mushrooms, soaked in hot tap water until softened,
    drained, stems trimmed, and caps cut into $^{1}/_{2}$-inch-wide slices
1 teaspoon dark sesame oil

1. Cut off and discard the skin from the duck breast. Slice the breast across the grain into ¼-inch-thick pieces, then cut them into pieces 2 inches long and 1 inch wide. Mix the duck, egg white, cornstarch, salt, and 1 tablespoon water in a medium bowl. Cover and refrigerate for 30 minutes.

2. Heat a large wok over high heat. Add enough oil to come about 1½ inches up the sides of the wok, and heat it to 325°F. Add the duck and stir gently, keeping the pieces separate and cooking until they turn pale brown, about 30 seconds. Add the water chestnuts and cook for 10 seconds. Using a wide wire-mesh strainer, transfer the duck and water chestnuts to a colander to drain. Discard all but 2 tablespoons of the oil from the wok.

3. To begin the sauce, mix the soy sauce, sugar, rice wine, vinegar, and stock in a small bowl, and set it aside. Dissolve the cornstarch in 1 tablespoon cold water in another small bowl, and set it aside.

4. Return the wok with the oil to medium-high heat. Add the scallions, garlic, and hot bean paste, and stir-fry until the garlic is fragrant, about 15 seconds. Add the pickled ginger and mushrooms, and stir-fry to blend the flavors, about 10 seconds. Stir in the soy sauce mixture, then the cornstarch mixture. Return the duck and water chestnuts to the wok, and stir-fry until the duck is just cooked through, about 20 seconds. Add the sesame oil, and serve immediately.

A SPECIAL-OCCASION FESTIVITY often requires an extraordinary dish, one that may take a bit of effort, but one that also guarantees that your guests know that they are being treated to something exceptional. This tea-smoked duck, with steps of marinating, smoking, steaming, and deep-frying, is such a dish. The duck—succulent and deeply flavored, with a crisp, burnished skin—is sliced and served in thin Chinese pancakes like its cousin, Beijing duck. The duck can be marinated, smoked, and steamed up to a day in advance; store it, covered, in the refrigerator, and it will be ready for frying right before serving. You will need a round wok or cake rack to fit in the wok to hold the duck while it is smoked.

Makes 4 to 8 servings

Tea-Smoked Duck Sichuan-Style

One 6-pound duck

Marinade

5 tablespoons salt
2 scallions, white and green parts, trimmed
Two 1/4-inch-thick slices peeled fresh ginger
3 Sichuan peppercorns
One 3-inch cinnamon stick
2 whole star anise

For smoking the duck

Vegetable oil
Aluminum foil, for lining the wok
1/4 cup sugar
1/4 cup oolong tea leaves
1/4 cup long-grain rice
1 tablespoon Sichuan peppercorns
One 3-inch cinnamon stick
2 whole star anise

Vegetable oil, for deep-frying

Dipping Sauce

$\frac{1}{2}$ cup hoisin sauce

$1\frac{1}{2}$ teaspoons rice wine or dry sherry

$1\frac{1}{2}$ teaspoons distilled white vinegar

$\frac{1}{2}$ teaspoon dark sesame oil

For serving the duck

1 cucumber, peeled and cut into very thin strips about $1\frac{1}{2}$ inches long

4 scallions, white and green parts, cut into very thin strips about $1\frac{1}{2}$ inches long

20 small Chinese pancakes

1. To marinate the duck: At least 1 day before serving the duck, cut off and discard the excess fat. Cut off and discard the neck and the tips of the wings. Discard the gizzards. Bring 1 quart of water to a boil in a saucepan. Add the salt, scallions, ginger, peppercorns, cinnamon stick, and star anise, and return to a boil. Pour the marinade into a nonreactive container that is large enough to hold the duck, and let it cool to room temperature.

2. Add the duck to the marinade, cover, and refrigerate for 24 hours, turning the duck after 12 hours. (The duck can also be marinated in a jumbo self-sealing plastic bag set in a large bowl.)

3. Drain the duck from the marinade and place it on a wire rack on a rimmed baking sheet. Position a large electric fan 18 inches from the rack, and train the fan on the duck. (If using a smaller fan, position it 12 inches from the rack.) Let the duck stand in front of the fan until the skin is dry, about 2 hours

4. Next, smoke the duck: Using a paper towel, lightly oil the inside of a wok with vegetable oil. Line the interior of the wok with aluminum foil, and lightly oil the foil. Mix the sugar, tea leaves, rice, peppercorns, cinnamon stick, and star anise in the wok. Place a round rack over the mixture. Arrange the duck on the rack, breast side up. Set the wok over high heat, and cover it. When smoke emerges, after about 1 minute, lower the heat to medium-high and continue smoking for 20 minutes. You should see a wisp of smoke emerging from the wok during this time, so adjust the heat as needed to keep the smoke visible. When done, the duck should be a burnished dark gold or light brown, not pale nor golden brown.

5. While the duck is smoking, fill the bottom half of an Asian-style steamer with about 4 inches of water, and bring it to a boil over high heat. You will need a heatproof bowl that will hold the duck and fit in the upper part of the steamer.

6. Transfer the duck to the bowl, place it in the upper part of the steamer, cover, and steam for 45 minutes. Transfer the duck to a colander to drain. (The duck can be prepared to this point, cooled, covered, and refrigerated for up to 1 day. Remove it from the refrigerator 1 hour before deep-frying. Otherwise, if the duck is ice-cold, it will make the oil bubble furiously.)

7. Heat a large wok over high heat. Add enough oil to come about 1½ inches up the sides of the wok, and heat it to 350°F. Gently lower the duck into the wok. Using a metal scoop, bathe the top of the duck with oil as it fries. Fry until it is golden brown on one side, about 5 minutes. Turn the duck over, and fry until golden brown on the other side, about 5 minutes. Transfer the duck to a colander to drain.

8. To make the dipping sauce, mix the hoisin sauce, rice wine, vinegar, and sesame oil in a small bowl. Stir well and set aside. Place the cucumber and scallions strips on a serving platter.

9. Reheat the water in the steamer (or, if making it the next day, refill a clean steamer) and bring to a boil. Place the pancakes on a plate that will fit in the top of the steamer, and steam, covered, until they are hot, about 2 minutes. (The pancakes can also be heated, separated with paper towels, in a microwave oven on high power for about 30 seconds.)

10. Place the duck on a cutting board. Using a cleaver or heavy knife, cut off the legs and wings, and transfer them to the serving platter. Cut the duck in half lengthwise, and cut each half into 8 pieces. Remove the meat from the bone. Serve immediately. To eat, put a teaspoon of the dipping sauce on a pancake, then a piece of boneless duck and some cucumber and scallions; then roll up the pancake.

Beef, Lamb, and Pork

*T*HE CHINESE do not eat much beef, partly out of Buddhist respect for the cow. Also, the cow is so useful in an agrarian culture that farmers believe it shouldn't be eaten. Some scholars have yet a third reason: From years spent pulling the plow, Chinese beef historically has been unpalatably tough. While beef in China is slowly improving, the quality of American beef has always been high, and beef dishes are very popular with our customers at Shun Lee.

The northern Chinese eat lots of lamb, from slowly simmered stews to stir-fries with vegetables. Our lamb rib chops are perfect for a dinner party.

In China pork tops the list of favorite protein foods, although chicken and beef are making inroads, especially among prosperous diners who eat out often. Pork belly, which is fresh, unsmoked bacon, is beloved for its melting texture, and it is worth searching out from a Chinese butcher. Pork butt is the preferred cut for stir-fries.

IN THIS SICHUANESE DISH, the minced beef represents the ants, and the broccoli stems are meant to be the tree. It is a light, refreshing dish, with just a sprinkling of meat, a handful of transparent noodles, and crisp-tender Chinese broccoli. Use broccoli florets instead of the Chinese variety, if you like.

Makes 4 servings

Ants Climbing a Tree

5 ounces flank steak, minced coarsely with a cleaver or in a food processor

$\frac{1}{2}$ large egg white (beat a whole egg white until foamy and measure out half)

$\frac{1}{4}$ cup plus 1 tablespoon rice wine or dry sherry

Vegetable oil, for passing through, plus 1 tablespoon

1 tablespoon cornstarch, plus 2 teaspoons

Pinch of salt

Pinch of ground white pepper

4 ounces bean threads (mung bean flour noodles)

$\frac{1}{4}$ cup soy sauce

1 teaspoon sugar

1 teaspoon hot bean paste

1 scallion, white and green parts, trimmed and minced

$\frac{1}{4}$ cup peeled and minced fresh ginger

4 Chinese dried black mushrooms, soaked in hot tap water until softened, stems trimmed, caps minced

$1\frac{1}{2}$ tablespoons seeded and minced red bell pepper

$1\frac{1}{2}$ cups Chicken Stock (page 70) or canned chicken broth

1 tablespoon dark sesame oil

8 ounces Chinese broccoli

1. Combine the steak, egg white, the 1 tablespoon rice wine, the 1 tablespoon vegetable oil, and the 1 tablespoon cornstarch, salt, and white pepper in a medium bowl. Add 1 tablespoon of water and mix well. Cover, and refrigerate for 30 minutes.

2. Bring a medium saucepan of water to a boil over high heat. Add the bean threads, and remove from the heat. Let stand until the bean threads have just softened to the texture of rubber bands, about 10 minutes. Drain in a wire strainer, and set aside.

3. Bring another saucepan of lightly salted water to a boil over high heat. Keep the water boiling so it is ready to cook the broccoli.

4. Heat a large wok over high heat. Add enough oil to come about 1 inch up the sides of the wok, and heat it to 325°F. Add the beef and stir gently until it turns light brown, about 40 seconds. Using a wide wire-mesh strainer, transfer the beef to a colander to drain. Discard all but 2 tablespoons of the oil from the wok.

5. Mix the soy sauce, sugar, and hot bean paste in a small bowl, and set it aside. Dissolve the 2 teaspoons cornstarch in 1 tablespoon water in a small bowl, and set aside.

6. Return the wok with the oil to high heat. Add the scallion and ginger, and stir-fry until fragrant, about 10 seconds. Add the mushrooms and bell pepper, and stir-fry for 10 seconds more. Add the steak, remaining ¼ cup rice wine, stock, and drained bean threads, and stir-fry for 20 seconds, turning the bean threads vigorously so that everything is thoroughly mixed. Add the soy sauce mixture and the cornstarch mixture and stir-fry until the liquid has nearly evaporated, about 2 to 3 minutes.

7. While the beef and bean thread mixture is cooking, add the broccoli to the boiling water and cook until crisp-tender, about 2 minutes. Drain in a colander.

8. Arrange the broccoli on a serving platter with the leafy parts at one end. Stir the sesame oil into the beef and bean thread mixture, and pour the mixture over the leafy part of the broccoli, letting the stems protrude so that they resemble tree trunks. Serve immediately.

WITH A WELL-STOCKED PANTRY of Chinese condiments and a quick stop at the market for a handful of fresh ingredients, this simple dinner dish can be on the table very quickly. It marries toothsome flank steak with crunchy sugar snap peas in a garlicky sauce.   **Makes 4 servings**

Beef with Sugar Snap Peas

12 ounces flank steak, cut into pieces $1\frac{1}{2}$ inches long, 1 inch wide, and $\frac{1}{4}$ inch thick
$\frac{1}{2}$ large egg white (beat a whole egg white and measure out half)
2 tablespoon rice wine or dry sherry
2 tablespoons cornstarch
Pinch of salt
Pinch of ground white pepper
Vegetable oil, for passing through, plus 1 tablespoon
6 ounces sugar snap peas, trimmed, or snow peas
2 ounces water chestnuts ($\frac{1}{3}$ to $\frac{1}{2}$ cup), sliced $\frac{1}{8}$ inch thick

Sauce
$\frac{1}{4}$ cup Chicken Stock (page 70) or canned chicken broth
2 tablespoons soy sauce
2 teaspoons oyster sauce
1 teaspoon sugar
1 tablespoon rice wine or sherry
$\frac{1}{2}$ teaspoon ground white pepper
1 tablespoon cornstarch

2 scallions, white and green parts, trimmed and sliced diagonally into $\frac{1}{2}$-inch pieces
4 garlic cloves, peeled and minced
1 teaspoon dark sesame oil

1. Mix the steak, egg white, rice wine, cornstarch, salt, pepper, and 2 tablespoons water in a medium bowl. Add the 1 tablespoon oil and mix again. Cover, and refrigerate for 30 minutes.

2. Heat a large wok over high heat. Add enough vegetable oil to come about 1 inch up the sides of the wok, and heat it to 325°F. Add the steak and stir gently until the meat turns light brown, about 40 seconds. Add the sugar snap peas and water chestnuts, and stir for 15 seconds. The vegetables will be crunchy. Using a wide wire-mesh

strainer, transfer the steak, sugar snap peas, and water chestnuts to a colander to drain. Discard all but 2 tablespoons of the oil from the wok.

3. To begin the sauce, mix the stock, soy sauce, oyster sauce, sugar, rice wine, and white pepper in a small bowl, and set it aside. Dissolve the cornstarch in 3 tablespoons cold water in another small bowl, and set it aside.

4. Return the wok with the oil to high heat. Add the scallions and garlic, and stir-fry until they are fragrant, about 10 seconds. Stir in the stock mixture, then the cornstarch mixture, and bring to a boil. Add the beef, sugar snap peas, and water chestnuts, and stir-fry for 15 seconds, making sure that the sauce evenly coats the meat and vegetables. Add the sesame oil, and serve immediately.

THE ORIGINAL SICHUAN RECIPE for this dish was for a cold, somewhat chewy appetizer of fried, dried, and shredded beef. It is a far cry from Shun Lee's Crispy Orange Beef, which was introduced in 1971, and which millions of Americans have since come to love.

Makes 4 servings

Crispy Orange Beef

8 ounces flank steak, cut into pieces 1 inch long,
$\frac{1}{2}$ inch wide, and $\frac{1}{4}$ inch thick
1$\frac{1}{2}$ teaspoons baking soda
1 orange

Sauce

2 tablespoons sugar
2 tablespoons red wine vinegar
1 tablespoon rice wine or dry sherry
1 tablespoon soy sauce
1 teaspoon cornstarch

Vegetable oil, for passing through
1 cup cornstarch
1 large egg white, lightly beaten
3 scallions, white part only, trimmed and sliced diagonally
into $\frac{1}{2}$-inch pieces ($\frac{1}{2}$ cup)
1 teaspoon dark sesame oil
1 tablespoon orange liqueur, such as Grand Marnier
$\frac{1}{4}$ teaspoon hot chili paste

1. Mix the flank steak, baking soda, and 3 tablespoons of water in a medium bowl. Cover, and refrigerate for 4 hours or overnight. (The baking soda will tenderize the steak.)

2. Using a vegetable peeler, remove the colored zest from the orange. Cut the zest into thin strips about 1 inch long, and set them aside. Save the orange flesh for another use.

3. To begin the sauce, mix the sugar, vinegar, rice wine, soy sauce, and cornstarch in a small bowl. Set it aside.

4. Heat a large wok over high heat. Add enough vegetable oil to come about $1\frac{1}{2}$ inches up the sides of the wok, and heat it to 375°F. Meanwhile, add the cornstarch and egg white to the steak, and mix well to coat the steak with the batter.

5. Add the flank steak to the oil, one piece at a time so it doesn't splash or stick together, and stir gently until it begins to look crispy, about 1 minute. Using a wide wire-mesh strainer, transfer the steak to a colander to drain. Using a fine-mesh wire strainer, remove any bits of fried batter from the wok.

6. Reheat the oil to 375°F, return the flank steak to the wok, and fry again until the beef is crispy all over, about 2 minutes. Transfer to a strainer to drain. Discard all but 1 tablespoon of the oil from the wok.

7. Return the wok with the oil to high heat. Add the scallions, flank steak, sugar-vinegar mixture, orange zest, sesame oil, Grand Marnier, and hot chili paste. Stir-fry until all of the ingredients are well-blended, about 30 seconds. Serve immediately.

IN CANTONESE, the word *kew* means "large chunk of meat." Beef Kew was a familiar item in Chinese restaurants during the '40s and '50s. For a more refined version, we use the most tender cut of beef, the luxurious filet mignon, and pair it with asparagus, a vegetable that is relatively new to China. But the secret is in the sauce, which is spicier than the original Cantonese recipe.   **Makes 4 servings**

Hunan Steak Kew

12 ounces filet mignon, cut across the grain into slices 2 inches long,
   1 inch wide, and $\frac{1}{4}$ inch thick
1 large egg white
2 tablespoons cornstarch
$\frac{1}{8}$ teaspoon salt
Vegetable oil, for passing through
6 asparagus stalks, tough ends discarded, spears peeled and sliced diagonally
   into $1\frac{1}{2}$-inch-long pieces

Sauce
3 tablespoons distilled white vinegar
3 tablespoons rice wine or dry sherry
3 tablespoons soy sauce
$2\frac{1}{2}$ tablespoons sugar
2 teaspoons hot chili paste
1 tablespoon cornstarch
3 tablespoons Chicken Stock (page 70) or canned chicken broth

2 scallions, white part only, trimmed and sliced diagonally into $\frac{1}{2}$-inch pieces
4 garlic cloves, peeled and sliced $\frac{1}{8}$ inch thick
1 teaspoon hot chili oil, optional

1. Mix the filet mignon, egg white, cornstarch, salt, and 1 tablespoon water in a medium bowl. Cover, and refrigerate for 30 minutes.

2. Heat a large wok over high heat. Add enough oil to come about $1\frac{1}{2}$ inches up the sides of the wok, and heat it to 325°F. Add the beef slices, one piece at a time to keep them from splashing oil and sticking together, and stir gently until they turn light brown, about 40 seconds. Add the asparagus and stir for 20 seconds. Transfer the beef and asparagus to a colander, and drain. Discard all but 2 tablespoons of the oil from the wok.

3. To begin the sauce, mix the vinegar, rice wine, soy sauce, sugar, and hot chili paste in a small bowl, and set it aside. Dissolve the cornstarch in the stock in another small bowl, and set it aside.

4. Return the wok with the oil to high heat. Add the scallions and garlic, and stir-fry until they are fragrant, about 10 seconds. Add the vinegar mixture and stir for 10 seconds. Then stir in the cornstarch mixture. Return the beef and asparagus to the wok, and stir-fry until they are evenly coated with the sauce, about 20 seconds. Add the hot chili oil, if using, in the last 5 seconds. Serve immediately.

INSPIRED BY chef Daniel Boulud's short ribs braised in red wine, I experimented using the traditional red-cooked technique that is popular in the ancient cities around Shanghai: Suzhou, Hangzhou, Yangzhou, and Wuxi. Red-cooking uses soy sauce and sugar, and traditionally the technique means braising the food, usually meat, until meltingly tender. The ribs are nestled on a bed of spinach. The meat is taken off the bones to allow diners to use chopsticks.   **Makes 2 to 4 servings**

Red-Cooked Beef Short Ribs

2 1/2 pounds beef short ribs, cut by the butcher into 8 pieces about 2 inches long
5 cups dry sherry or red wine
1/2 cup sugar
1/2 cup soy sauce
2 scallions, white and green parts, trimmed
One 1 1/2-inch piece peeled fresh ginger, flattened with a cleaver
Two 3-inch cinnamon sticks
3 dried small hot red chilies
3 whole star anise
1 teaspoon ground white pepper
1 pound spinach

1. Bring a large saucepan of water to a boil over high heat. Add the short ribs and cook for 1 minute to remove some of the surface fat. Drain in a colander.

2. Combine the sherry, sugar, soy sauce, scallions, ginger, cinnamon sticks, chilies, star anise, white pepper, and 3 cups of water in a flameproof casserole. Stir to mix. Add the short ribs, cover, and bring to a boil over high heat. Reduce the heat to medium-low, cover, and simmer until the meat is fork-tender, about 2 1/2 hours.

3. Using a slotted spoon, transfer the short ribs to a chopping board. Cut the meat from the bones, transfer the meat to a bowl, and discard the bones. Remove the scallions, ginger, and whole spices from the sauce. Boil the sauce, uncovered, until it is syrupy, glossy, and reduced to 3/4 cup, about 15 minutes.

4. Meanwhile, bring a large pot of lightly salted water to a boil over high heat. Add the spinach and cook until tender, about 1 1/2 minutes. Drain in a colander. Place the spinach on a platter.

5. Return the short rib meat to the casserole and cook to heat through. Spoon the meat and sauce over the spinach, and serve immediately.

THIS SIMPLE, LIGHT SICHUAN home-style dish offers unique textures because all the ingredients are shredded. There are so many chilies at the market these days: be as adventurous in your selection as your heat tolerance will allow. Start with a mildly hot green pepper, such as Anaheim, or Hungarian or Italian frying peppers, and increase the heat with smaller, hotter candidates like cayenne or serrano chilies. Even a mix of green and red bell peppers with a single chili works for more timid palates.

Makes 4 servings

Shredded Beef with Fresh Hot Peppers

12 ounces flank steak

2 tablespoons plus 2 teaspoons rice wine or dry sherry

$1/2$ large egg (beat the egg until foamy, then measure out half)

Pinch of ground white pepper

Pinch of salt

2 tablespoons cornstarch

Vegetable oil, for passing through, plus 1 tablespoon

$1/3$ cup sliced canned bamboo shoots (cut 2 inches long and $1/8$ inch thick)

3 tablespoons soy sauce

2 teaspoons sugar

About 6 ounces assorted fresh hot peppers and chilies, mixed according to taste
    (see headnote), seeds and ribs removed, cut into thin 2-inch-long shreds ($1/2$ cup)

1 leek, white part only, trimmed and cut into thin strips
    about 2 inches long, well washed

5 garlic cloves, peeled and sliced $1/8$ inch thick

1 teaspoon dark sesame oil

1. Freeze the steak until it is partially frozen but can still be cut with a knife, about 1 hour, depending on the thickness of the steak and the freezer temperature. Cut the steak across the grain into $1/4$-inch-thick slices. Stack a few steak slices and cut them in half crosswise, then lengthwise into $1/4$-inch-thick strips. Repeat with all the steak.

2. Mix the steak strips, 2 tablespoons rice wine, egg, white pepper, and salt in a medium bowl. Add 2 tablespoons water, 1 tablespoon of the cornstarch, and the 1 tablespoon oil, and mix again. Cover, and refrigerate for 30 minutes.

3. Heat a large wok over high heat. Add enough oil to come about 1½ inches up the sides of the wok and heat it to 325°F. Carefully add the steak, taking care that the pieces don't splash or stick to each other, and stir gently until they turn light brown, about 40 seconds. Add the bamboo shoots and stir-fry for 20 seconds. Using a wide wire-mesh strainer, transfer the steak and bamboo shoots to a colander to drain. Discard all but 2 tablespoons of the oil from the wok.

4. Mix the soy sauce, sugar, and remaining 2 teaspoons rice wine in a small bowl, and set it aside. Dissolve the remaining 1 tablespoon cornstarch in 3 tablespoons cold water in another small bowl, and set it aside.

5. Return the wok with the oil to high heat. Add the peppers and chilies, leek, and garlic, and stir-fry until the peppers are crisp-tender, about 1 minute. Return the steak and bamboo shoots to the wok, add the soy sauce mixture, and stir-fry until the beef is heated through, about 20 seconds. Add the cornstarch mixture and stir-fry until the sauce thickens, about 10 seconds. Add the sesame oil, and serve immediately.

LAMB STEW HAS MANY INCARNATIONS in many cuisines, and some of them are very rustic indeed. This red-cooked Chinese rendition, bolstered with unusual dried bean threads, is hardly ordinary. For the most succulent results, look for lamb breast at a Chinese butcher shop. Lacking that, use 1-inch chunks of boneless lamb shoulder or boneless leg of lamb. And when purchasing the dried bean threads, do not confuse them with transparent mung bean threads: look for yellowish dried noodles that resemble bunches of parchment. When fried and soaked, the bean threads have a lovely, slightly chewy-tender texture.

Makes 4 servings

Beijing Lamb Stew

1 pound boneless lamb breast, chopped into 1-inch cubes
Vegetable oil, for deep-frying, plus $1/4$ cup
2 ounces (about $1 1/2$ bunches) dried soybean threads
2 scallions, white part only, trimmed and sliced into 1-inch pieces
One 1-inch piece peeled fresh ginger, cut into
    pieces $1/2$ inch square and $1/4$ inch thick
2 small dried hot red chilies
2 tablespoons rice wine or dry sherry
2 whole star anise
One $1 1/2$-inch piece of cinnamon stick
3 tablespoons soy sauce
$1/4$ cup smashed rock sugar
1 medium carrot, peeled and cut into $1 1/2$-inch-long wedges
6 Chinese dried black mushrooms (about $1/2$ cup), soaked, trimmed,
    each mushroom cut into 3 pieces
1 cube red fermented bean curd, optional

1. Bring a large saucepan of water to a boil over high heat. Add the lamb and cook to remove some of the surface fat, about 3 minutes. Drain in a colander. Place the lamb on a plate and set it aside.

2. Clean the saucepan, fill it with water, and bring it to a boil over high heat. Keep the water boiling so it is ready for the bean threads.

3. Heat a large wok over high heat. Add enough oil to come about 1 inch up the sides of the wok, and heat it to 325°F. Carefully add the bean threads, and cook until they turn golden-brown, about 10 seconds. Using a wide wire-mesh strainer, transfer them to a colander to drain. Turn off the heat under the wok. Add the fried bean threads to the boiling water, turn off the heat, and let them soak until softened, about 1 minute. Drain in a colander. Place the bean threads on a cutting board, cut them into 1½-inch-long pieces, and set them aside. Discard the oil from the wok.

4. Add ¼ cup oil to a flameproof casserole or Dutch oven and heat over high heat. Add the scallions, ginger, and dried chilies, and stir-fry until they are fragrant, about 15 seconds. Add the lamb and stir-fry until the lamb is browned, about 2½ minutes. Stir in the rice wine, star anise, and cinnamon stick, then the soy sauce, rock sugar, and 3 cups of water, and bring to a boil. Reduce the heat to medium-low. Cover the wok and simmer at a gentle bubble for 40 minutes. Add the bean threads, cover, and continue simmering for 20 minutes.

5. Add the carrot, mushrooms, and fermented bean curd, if using, to the wok. Mash the bean curd on the side of the wok and stir it into the sauce. Simmer, covered, for 15 minutes, until the lamb and carrots are tender. (The stew can be made up to 1 day ahead, cooled, covered, and refrigerated. Scrape off and discard the solidified fat from the surface. Reheat gently before serving.)

6. Skim off and discard the fat from the surface of the sauce. Remove the star anise, cinnamon, and chilies, and serve hot.

SHUN LEE INTRODUCED LAMB to its menu in 1972, and since then other Chinese restaurants have followed suit. Here, tender slices of meat from the lamb leg are bound with scallions and leeks in a spicy, garlicky sauce.   **Makes 4 servings**

Hunan Lamb with Scallions

1 pound boneless leg of lamb, trimmed
1 large egg
1$\frac{1}{2}$ tablespoons cornstarch
Vegetable oil, for passing through
$\frac{1}{4}$ cup canned sliced bamboo shoots (cut into thin 1$\frac{1}{2}$-inch-long strips)

Sauce

3 tablespoons rice wine or dry sherry
2 tablespoons soy sauce
2 tablespoons sugar
2 tablespoons distilled white vinegar
1 tablespoon hot bean paste
Pinch of ground white pepper
1$\frac{1}{2}$ teaspoons cornstarch

1 leek, white part only, trimmed and cut into thin
    1$\frac{1}{2}$-inch-long strips, well washed
5 garlic cloves, peeled and sliced $\frac{1}{8}$ inch thick
4 scallions, white and green parts, trimmed and sliced
    diagonally into $\frac{1}{4}$-inch pieces

1. Cut the lamb across the grain into $\frac{1}{4}$-inch-thick slices. Cut the slices into pieces about 2 inches long and 1 inch wide. Mix the lamb with the egg, cornstarch, and 1 tablespoon water in a medium bowl. Cover, and refrigerate for 30 minutes.

2. Heat a large wok over high heat. Add enough oil to come about 1 inch up the sides of the wok, and heat it to 325°F. Add the lamb carefully, so the pieces don't splash or stick to each other, and stir gently until they turn light brown, about 30 seconds. Add the bamboo shoots and stir for 20 seconds. Using a wide wire-mesh strainer, transfer the lamb and bamboo shoots to a colander to drain. Discard all but 2 tablespoons of the oil from the wok.

3. To begin the sauce, mix the rice wine, soy sauce, sugar, vinegar, hot bean paste, and white pepper in a small bowl, and set it aside. Dissolve the cornstarch in 2 tablespoons cold water in another small bowl, and set it aside.

4. Return the wok with the oil to high heat. Add the leek and garlic, and stir-fry until the garlic is fragrant, about 15 seconds. Return the lamb and bamboo shoots to the wok; then add the scallions and the rice wine mixture, and stir-fry for 10 seconds. Add the cornstarch mixture and stir-fry until the lamb turns a dark brown and the sauce has evenly coated the meat and vegetables, about 20 seconds. Serve immediately.

WHILE MOST OF THE RECIPES in this book are meant to be eaten Chinese-style, with chopsticks, this nontraditional dish requires a fork and knife.

Makes 4 servings

Grilled Lamb Rib Chops with Garlic and Ginger

8 baby lamb rib chops (about 4 ounces each)
2 tablespoons rice wine or dry sherry
1 teaspoon salt
$\frac{1}{2}$ teaspoon freshly ground black pepper
24 broccoli florets
2 medium carrots, peeled, each cut into six 1-inch-long wedges

Sauce

$\frac{1}{2}$ cup Chicken Stock (page 70) or canned chicken broth
$\frac{1}{4}$ cup rice wine or dry sherry
2 tablespoons soy sauce
2 tablespoons distilled white vinegar
2 tablespoons sugar
2 teaspoons oyster sauce
$\frac{1}{4}$ teaspoon freshly ground black pepper
1 tablespoon cornstarch

$\frac{1}{4}$ cup vegetable oil
6 scallions, white and green parts, trimmed and sliced diagonally into 1-inch pieces
6 garlic cloves, peeled and sliced $\frac{1}{8}$ inch thick
2 tablespoons hot chili paste
2 tablespoons dark sesame oil

1. Using the flat side of a cleaver, flatten the lamb chops slightly. Combine the lamb chops with the rice wine, salt, and pepper in a large bowl. Cover, and refrigerate for 30 minutes.

2. Position a broiler rack about 3 inches from the heat source, and preheat the broiler. (The top of the chops should be about 1$\frac{1}{2}$ inches from the heat.) Remove the lamb

chops from the marinade. Broil the chops until browned, about 4 minutes. Turn and cook until the other side is browned and the chops are medium-rare, about 2 minutes longer. Transfer the chops to a plate and tent with aluminum foil to keep warm.

3. Meanwhile, bring a medium saucepan of lightly salted water to a boil. Add the broccoli and carrots, and cook until they are brightly colored but still crisp, about 2 minutes. Drain in colander. Arrange on a serving platter, and tent with aluminum foil to keep warm.

4. To begin the sauce, mix the stock, rice wine, soy sauce, vinegar, sugar, oyster sauce, and pepper in a small bowl, and set it aside. Dissolve the cornstarch in 3 tablespoons cold water in another small bowl, and set it aside.

5. Heat a large wok over high heat. Add the oil and heat until it shimmers. Add the scallions and garlic, and stir-fry until the garlic is fragrant, about 20 seconds. Add the stock mixture, chili paste, and sesame oil, and cook for 15 seconds. Add the cornstarch mixture and bring to a boil. Add the chops, mix thoroughly, and cook just to heat the lamb, about 20 seconds. Place the chops on the platter, arranging them with the bones up, crisscrossed like a tepee, over the carrots and broccoli. Serve immediately.

PORK BELLY, from the underside of the pig, has made its way onto restaurant menus of many different cuisines, from Italian and French to Chinese, and it deserves to be served at your house, too. At first diners at Shun Lee seemed wary of this fatty cut, but once they became familiar with its unctuous texture and great flavor, they warmed up to it. Inexpensive pork belly can be found at ethnic markets. If you can't find it, use 1-inch chunks of boneless pork shoulder. This dish honors Su Tung-po, a Sung-dynasty poet who lived in Hangzhou and whose cook made him this dish, his favorite.

If you do not want to eat the skin with the layer of fat, remove the skin and just eat the meat. The cognoscenti, however, love the skin. Adding the last tablespoon of sugar at the end makes the sauce shinier. **Makes 4 servings**

Hangzhou Braised Pork

2 pounds pork belly, cut into eight 2-inch-square pieces
2 scallions, white and green parts, trimmed and cut into thirds
1 cup rice wine or dry sherry
$\frac{1}{3}$ cup plus 1 tablespoon sugar
$\frac{1}{4}$ cup plus 2 tablespoons soy sauce
One 1-inch piece peeled fresh ginger, cut into 5 slices
1 teaspoon ground white pepper
3 whole star anise
One 1$\frac{1}{2}$-inch piece of cinnamon stick
5 small dried hot red chilies
1 pound spinach

1. Bring a large saucepan of water to a boil over high heat. Add the pork and cook to remove some of the surface fat, about 3 minutes. Drain in a colander. Rinse the pork under cold running water for 1 minute.

2. Place the scallions on the bottom of a flameproof casserole or Dutch oven (this keeps the pork from sticking to the bottom), and top with the pork. Add 3 cups water, the rice wine, the $\frac{1}{3}$ cup sugar, the $\frac{1}{4}$ cup soy sauce, and the ginger, white pepper, star anise, cinnamon stick, and dried chilies. Bring to a boil over high heat. Reduce the heat to medium-low, cover, and simmer gently until the pork is very tender, about 2 hours.

3. Meanwhile, bring a large saucepan of lightly salted water to a boil over high heat, and reduce the heat to low to keep the water simmering.

4. Transfer the pork to a cutting board. Cut the meat from the bones, and discard the bones. Using a slotted spoon, remove and discard the ginger, scallions, star anise, cinnamon stick, and chilies from the sauce. Increase the heat to high and boil the sauce, uncovered, until it becomes syrupy, about 7 minutes.

5. While the sauce is reducing, return the saucepan of water to a boil. Add the spinach and cook just until it is wilted and bright green, about 1 minute. Drain well in a colander. Spread the spinach on a platter.

6. Add the pork, the remaining 2 tablespoons soy sauce, and the remaining 1 tablespoon sugar to the sauce, and return it to a boil.

7. Using a slotted spoon, transfer the pork, skin side up, to the center of the platter. Spoon the sauce on top, and serve immediately.

THESE BRAISED RIBS are from the city of Wuxi, a textile center about 150 miles west of Shanghai. The ribs have a complex flavor with hints of sweetness (rock sugar), spice (hot peppers), and wine (fermented red rice). They are yet another version of a red-cooked dish. The fermented red rice contributes its special, musky, winey flavor—and its deep scarlet color.

Makes 4 servings

Baby Ribs Wuxi-Style

1½ pounds baby back pork spareribs, cut lengthwise into individual ribs
   and then crosswise into about 20 pieces, each 1½ to 2 inches long
¼ cup rice wine or dry sherry
⅓ cup smashed rock sugar
¼ cup soy sauce
¼ cup fermented red rice, loosely tied in a piece of cheesecloth (see Note)
4 scallions, white and green parts, trimmed
One ½-inch piece peeled fresh ginger, smashed under a cleaver
2 whole star anise
One 3-inch cinnamon stick
4 small dried hot red chilies

1. Bring a large pot of water to a boil over high heat. Add the ribs and cook to remove some of the surface fat, about 2 minutes. Drain in a colander.

2. Mix 2 cups water with the rice wine, rock sugar, soy sauce, fermented red rice, scallions, ginger, star anise, cinnamon stick, and chilies in a flameproof casserole or Dutch oven. Add the ribs and bring to a boil over high heat. Place a plate or a flat lid inside the wok to keep the ribs submerged in the sauce. Partially cover the casserole with the lid. Reduce the heat to medium-low, and cook at a steady simmer until the ribs are tender and the sauce is syrupy, 35 to 40 minutes. If the sauce seems too thin, transfer the ribs to a platter, cover them with aluminum foil to keep warm, and boil the sauce over high heat for a few minutes to reduce it. Remove the star anise, cinnamon stick, and chilies. Transfer the ribs and sauce to a serving platter, and serve immediately. (The red rice is only a seasoning, and should not be eaten.)

Note: Fermented rice, like regular rice, will triple in volume when cooked, so tie it loosely in cheesecloth so it has room to expand.

LIKE ANTS CLIMB A TREE, this dish of pork meatballs and cabbage is pictur-esquely named. The lion's head is the meatball, and its mane the leafy cabbage. Tenderness is the way to judge the quality of Lion's Head: traditional cooks use very fatty pork to add juiciness; others use bean curd for its softness. I mix pork and bean curd, and the results are excellent. This soothing dish is perfect family fare.

Makes 4 servings

Lion's Head with Cabbage

Meatballs

    1 block (8 ounces) firm bean curd, drained
    10 ounces ground pork
    1 scallion, white and green parts, trimmed and minced
    1 large egg, beaten
    1/2 teaspoon salt
    1 tablespoon cornstarch
    Vegetable oil, for passing through

Sauce

    3 cups Chicken Stock (page 70) or canned chicken broth
    1/4 cup rice wine or dry sherry
    1/4 cup soy sauce
    2 scallions, white and green parts, trimmed and cut in half
    One 1-inch piece peeled fresh ginger, cut into 3 slices
    1 tablespoon sugar
    1/2 teaspoon ground white pepper

    12 ounces (12 leaves) Napa cabbage, cut into pieces 4 inches long and 2 inches wide
    1/4 cup sliced bamboo shoots (cut into pieces 2 inches long and 1/4 inch thick)
    4 Chinese dried black mushrooms, soaked in hot tap water until softened,
        stems trimmed, each cap cut in half
    1 tablespoon cornstarch

1. To make the meatballs, using the flat side of a cleaver, mash the bean curd flat and then mince it finely. Lightly mix the pork, scallion, egg, and salt in a medium bowl. Add the bean curd and lightly mix again. Add the cornstarch and mix just until combined. (Overhandling makes tough meatballs, so use a light touch, as the next step will combine the ingredients more.)

2. Using your hands, pick up a quarter of the pork mixture and throw it against the rest of the mixture in the bowl. This will help the pork mixture adhere and not fall apart in the cooking. Repeat 10 times. (It's fun. It's the food equivalent of slapping a softball into a catcher's glove.) Repeat with the remaining pork mixture.

3. Heat a large wok over high heat. Add enough oil to come about $1\frac{1}{2}$ inches up the sides of the wok, and heat it to 325°F. Form the pork mixture into 4 meatballs, and gently lower them into the wok. Fry in gently bubbling oil, carefully turning them once or twice, until golden on all sides, about 3 minutes. Using a wide wire-mesh strainer, transfer the meatballs to a colander to drain. Discard the oil. Rinse out the wok and dry it completely.

4. To begin the sauce, combine the stock, rice wine, soy sauce, scallions, ginger, sugar, and white pepper in the wok, and stir.

5. Add the meatballs, cabbage, bamboo shoots, and mushrooms to the wok, and bring to a boil over high heat. Cover the wok and reduce the heat to medium-low. Simmer until the meatballs are cooked through, about 30 minutes.

6. Dissolve the cornstarch in 3 tablespoons cold water in a small bowl, and stir into the sauce. Cook until the sauce thickens lightly, about 30 seconds. Serve immediately.

MU SHU PORK is associated with northern China—nearly all dishes that are wrapped in pancakes or are eaten with bread originated there. It is a dish that has many textures and flavors, with the crunch of the bamboo shoots, the softness of the scrambled egg, and the silky firmness of the tree ears. It can be served as a light one-dish meal. For the best results, use only the cabbage stems, as the leafy parts give off juices that will make the pancake soggy. A dab of hoisin sauce, spread on the pancake, is all the sauce you'll need.

If you cannot find dried lily buds, double the amount of tree ears.

Makes 4 servings

Mu Shu Pork

4 ounces fresh ham or boneless pork butt, cut into thin strips 2 inches long,
   $1/4$ inch wide, and $1/4$ inch thick
2 large eggs plus $1/2$ large egg white (beat a whole egg white
   until foamy and measure out half)
$1/4$ teaspoon plus a pinch of salt
$11/2$ teaspoons cornstarch
Vegetable oil, for passing through
2 tablespoons soy sauce
1 tablespoon rice wine or dry sherry
$1/4$ teaspoon dark sesame oil
10 ounces (12 leaves) Napa cabbage, stem part only
   (save the leafy parts for another use, such as a vegetable-stir fry),
   cut into pieces 2 inches long, $1/4$ inch wide, and $1/4$ inch thick
$1/4$ cup dried tree ears, soaked in hot tap water until softened,
   drained, patted dry, and torn by hand into 1-inch pieces
2 ounces dried lily buds, soaked in hot tap water until softened (see Note)
$1/4$ cup thinly sliced canned bamboo shoots (cut about 2 inches long)
3 scallions, green part only, trimmed and minced
8 small mu shu (also called Mandarin) pancakes, about 4 inches in diameter,
   or 4 large mu shu pancakes, about 8 inches in diameter
Hoisin sauce, for serving

1. Mix the pork with the egg white, pinch of salt, cornstarch, and $11/2$ teaspoons of water in a medium bowl until blended. Cover, and refrigerate for 30 minutes.

2. Fill the bottom of an Asian-style steamer with an inch or two of water, and bring it to a boil over high heat. (A collapsible Western-style steamer set in a large saucepan with $1/2$ inch of water works well, too.)

3. Heat a large wok over high heat. Add enough oil to come 1 inch up the sides of the wok, and heat it to 325°F. Add the pork and stir gently until it turns light brown, about 30 seconds. Using a wide wire-mesh strainer, transfer the pork to a colander to drain. Discard all but 2 tablespoons of the oil from the wok, and return the wok to high heat. Beat the whole eggs in a bowl until frothy, and add them to the wok. Scramble the eggs until they are quite firm and not runny, about 15 seconds. Transfer the eggs to the colander, separate from the pork, to drain.

4. Mix the soy sauce, rice wine, sesame oil, and remaining $1/4$ teaspoon salt in a small bowl, and set it aside.

5. Place the pancakes in the steamer and cover it. Heat until they are hot, about 2 minutes.

6. While the pancakes are warming, return the wok to high heat. Add the cabbage and stir-fry until softened, about 1 minute. Add the tree ears, lily buds, and bamboo shoots, and stir-fry for 20 seconds. If the cabbage discards liquid, tilt the wok over a colander and pour off the liquid. Return the pork to the wok, and add the scallions and the soy sauce mixture. Stir-fry for 30 seconds. At the last second, return the scrambled eggs to the wok and scatter them gently, so they remain yellow, among the pork mixture.

7. Place the pork mixture on a serving platter, surrounded by the pancakes. Serve immediately, with hoisin sauce on the side. Let each guest spread the sauce on a pancake, add the pork mixture, and roll up to eat.

Note: Any unused dried lily buds can be stored in a plastic bag in the refrigerator for up to 1 month.

THIS SICHUAN DISH features a regional sauce, sometimes called "fish-fragrant flavor," that combines hot chili paste, garlic, ginger, scallions, vinegar, sugar, and soy sauce—but no fish!

Makes 4 to 6 servings

Shredded Pork with Garlic Sauce

8 ounces fresh ham or pork butt, cut into pieces 2 inches long,
$\frac{1}{4}$ inch wide, and $\frac{1}{4}$ inch thick
1 large egg white
1 teaspoon cornstarch
$\frac{1}{8}$ teaspoon salt
Vegetable oil, for passing through

Sauce

3 tablespoons distilled white vinegar
3 tablespoons soy sauce
3 tablespoons sugar
2 tablespoons rice wine or dry sherry
1 tablespoon cornstarch

One $\frac{1}{2}$-inch piece peeled fresh ginger, minced
3 garlic cloves, sliced $\frac{1}{8}$ inch thick
2 scallions, white part only, cut into thin 2-inch-long strips
$\frac{1}{2}$ cup canned sliced bamboo shoots (cut into thin 2-inch-long strips)
$\frac{1}{2}$ cup sliced water chestnuts
$\frac{1}{2}$ cup dried tree ears, soaked in hot tap water until softened,
drained, patted dry, and torn by hand into 1-inch pieces
$\frac{1}{2}$ medium red bell pepper, seeds and ribs removed,
cut into thin 2-inch-long strips
$1\frac{1}{2}$ tablespoons hot chili paste
1 teaspoon hot chili oil, optional
1 teaspoon dark sesame oil

1. Combine the pork, egg white, cornstarch, salt, and 1 tablespoon of water in a medium bowl. Cover, and refrigerate for 30 minutes.

2. Heat a large wok over high heat. Add enough vegetable oil to come about 1 inch up the sides of the wok, and heat it to 325°F. Add the pork and stir gently until it turns light brown, about 40 seconds. Using a wide wire-mesh strainer, transfer the pork to a colander to drain. Discard all but 4 tablespoons of the oil from the wok.

3. To start the sauce, mix the vinegar, soy sauce, sugar, and rice wine in a small bowl, and set it aside. Dissolve the cornstarch in 3 tablespoons cold water, and set it aside.

4. Return the wok to high heat. Add the ginger, garlic, and scallions, and stir-fry until they are fragrant, about 15 seconds. Add the bamboo shoots, water chestnuts, tree ears, and bell pepper, and stir-fry until the bell pepper starts to soften, about 30 seconds. Transfer the vegetables to the colander. Add the vinegar mixture to the wok and stir for 10 seconds. Then add the hot chili paste and stir for 10 seconds more. Return the pork and vegetables to the wok, and stir-fry until the sauce comes a boil and thickens, about 20 seconds. Add the hot chili oil, if using, and stir-fry for 10 seconds. Add the sesame oil and serve immediately.

THIS SIMPLE AND HOMEY CANTONESE dish has a hundred variations. At Shun Lee we top it with salty duck eggs, but it can also be made with preserved sausages, sliced ham, or mushrooms. Since it is a somewhat salty dish, serve it with rice.

Makes 4 servings

Steamed Pork Patty with Duck Eggs

1 pound boneless fresh ham or pork butt

2 scallions, white part only, trimmed and minced

4 water chestnuts, minced

1 large egg, beaten

2 teaspoons peeled and minced fresh ginger

1 tablespoon rice wine or dry sherry

1 teaspoon salt

$\frac{1}{2}$ teaspoon sugar

$\frac{1}{2}$ teaspoon ground white pepper

4 salty duck eggs (see page 6)

1. Cut the pork crosswise into thin slices, then into thin strips. Using two cleavers, one in each hand, mince the pork. (Or pulse the pork strips in a food processor until minced.) Combine the pork with the scallions, water chestnuts, egg, ginger, rice wine, salt, sugar, and white pepper in a medium bowl.

2. Fill the bottom of an Asian steamer with 2 inches of water and bring to a boil over high heat. Choose a heatproof ceramic bowl to fit in the top of the steamer. Place the pork mixture in the bowl, and shape it into a patty about $1\frac{1}{2}$ inches thick. Using your fingers, make four round, shallow indentations in the meat patty, an equal distance apart, to hold the duck egg yolks. Gently crack a duck egg, making sure to keep the yolk whole, and place a yolk in an indentation. Pour the white over the patty. Repeat with the other 3 eggs, but discard the whites from the last 2 eggs, or the dish may be too salty.

3. Place the bowl in the top of the steamer, and cover. Steam over high heat until the patty is cooked through and shows no sign of pink, about 20 minutes. Be flexible with the timing, and cook a few minutes longer if necessary. Serve immediately.

THE SECRET INGREDIENT in this Sichuan dish is Ruey Fah Steam Powder, a combination of coarsely ground uncooked rice with ground cinnamon, cumin, star anise, and pepper. McCormick's Sichuan-style Fen Zheng Rou Seasoning is an acceptable substitute.

The dish looks intriguing, with its fluffy coating of spiced steamed rice, and the flavor is subtle, complex, and savory. It is perhaps even better the second day.

Makes 2 to 4 servings

Steamed Baby Ribs with Rice Flour

1 pound baby back pork spareribs, cut lengthwise into individual ribs and
    chopped with a cleaver into 1-inch pieces
1 scallion, white and green parts, trimmed and minced
1 tablespoon soy sauce
1 tablespoon rice wine or dry sherry
1 tablespoon vegetable oil
1 teaspoon dark sesame oil
1 teaspoon peeled and minced fresh ginger
$\frac{1}{2}$ teaspoon ground white pepper
1 teaspoon hot chili paste
$\frac{1}{4}$ teaspoon salt
One 1.76-ounce package Ruey Fah Steam Powder (see Note)

1. Combine the ribs, scallion, soy sauce, rice wine, vegetable oil, sesame oil, ginger, white pepper, hot chili paste, and salt in a large bowl. Cover, and refrigerate for 1 hour.

2. Fill the bottom of an Asian-style steamer with 2 inches of water and bring it to a boil over high heat. Choose a heatproof ceramic bowl to fit in the top of the steamer. Place the ribs in the bowl, sprinkle with the Steam Powder, and mix well to coat. Place the bowl in the steamer, and cover. Steam with a full head of steam until the ribs are tender, about 1 hour, adding hot water as necessary. Serve immediately.

Note: The secret ingredient is available in different forms; they are all interchangeable, and all will have "Steam Powder" on the label. McCormick's Sichuan-style Fen Zheng Rou Seasoning comes in a 1.42-ounce package, and Ruey Fah Steam Powder usually comes in 1.76-ounce packages. They are interchangeable—the extra .30 ounce won't make a difference in the dish.

BEIJING, SHANGHAI, AND OF COURSE CANTON all have their versions of a sweet-and-sour pork dish, but it was the Cantonese version, with ketchup and bell peppers, that became so popular in Chinese-American restaurants. Although other sweet-and-sour dishes have replaced this standard, it is still fun to make—and to eat   **Makes 4 servings**

Sweet-and-Sour Pork

12 ounces boneless pork butt
1 cup all-purpose flour
1 large egg
Vegetable oil, for deep-frying
$\frac{1}{2}$ small red bell pepper, seeds and ribs removed, cut into 1-inch squares
$\frac{1}{2}$ medium onion, peeled and cut into 4 wedges
$\frac{1}{2}$ cup ketchup
$\frac{1}{2}$ cup sugar
$\frac{1}{2}$ cup distilled white vinegar
2 tablespoons rice wine or dry sherry
$\frac{1}{4}$ teaspoon salt
$1\frac{1}{2}$ tablespoons cornstarch
4 canned peeled lychees, each cut in half
Eight $\frac{1}{2}$-inch-thick slices fresh pineapple, peeled, cored, and cut into pieces 1 inch long and $\frac{1}{2}$ inch wide

1. Cut the pork crosswise into $\frac{3}{4}$-inch-thick slices. Pound the slices with the flat side of a meat mallet until about $\frac{1}{2}$ inch thick. Cut into pieces about 1 inch square. Mix the flour, $\frac{3}{4}$ cup of water, and the egg in a medium bowl. Add the pork and mix well.

2. Heat a large wok over high heat. Add enough oil to come about 2 inches up the sides of the wok, and heat it to 375°F. Add the pork, one piece at a time so the pieces don't splash or stick to each other, and fry until golden brown, about 1 minute. Using a wide wire-mesh strainer, transfer the pork to a colander to drain.

3. Reheat the oil to 375°F. Return the pork to the wok and fry until crisp, about $2\frac{1}{2}$ minutes. Using the strainer, transfer the pork to the colander to drain again. Discard all but 2 tablespoons of the oil from the wok. Add the bell pepper and onion, and fry

Sweet-and-Sour Pork (continued)

until they begin to soften, about 30 seconds. Using the strainer, transfer the pepper and onion to the colander to drain.

4. Combine the ketchup, sugar, vinegar, rice wine, and salt in a small bowl, and set it aside. Dissolve the cornstarch in ¼ cup cold water in another small bowl, and set it aside.

5. Return the wok with the oil to high heat, add the ketchup mixture, and bring to a boil. Return the pork, bell pepper, and onion to the wok, and then add the lychees and pineapple. Add the cornstarch mixture and stir-fry until the pork is coated with sauce, about 20 seconds. Serve immediately.

IN THE AUTHENTIC SICHUAN VERSION of this dish, pork belly is boiled, sliced, and fried, but lean pork butt works, too. This rendition, inspired by the flavors of Shanghai, has a touch of sweetness from hoisin sauce. **Makes 4 servings**

Twice-Cooked Pork

10 ounces boneless pork butt
6 ounces (8 leaves) Napa cabbage, cut into pieces 2 inches long
    and 1½ inches wide
Vegetable oil, for passing through

Sauce

2 tablespoons hoisin sauce
2 tablespoons soy sauce
2 tablespoons rice wine or dry sherry
1 tablespoon sugar
1 tablespoon distilled white vinegar
2 teaspoons hot bean paste
1 teaspoon cornstarch

2 scallions, white part only, trimmed and sliced diagonally into ½-inch pieces
1 leek, white part only, trimmed and cut into thin 1½-inch-long strips, well washed
3 garlic cloves, peeled and sliced ⅛ inch thick
1 small hot fresh chili, such as Thai or serrano, seeds and ribs removed, cut into thin
    1½-inch-long strips
2 teaspoons hot chili oil, optional
1 teaspoon dark sesame oil

1. Bring 4 cups of water to a boil in a medium saucepan over high heat. Add the pork and return to a boil. Reduce the heat to medium-low and simmer, uncovered, until the pork is about 85 percent cooked (when sliced, it should have a pale pink center), about 15 minutes. Transfer the pork to a cutting board and let it cool. Then cut it crosswise into ⅛-inch-thick slices, and cut the slices into pieces about 1½ inches long and 1 inch wide.

2. Return the saucepan of the pork-cooking water to high heat. Add 2 more cups of water and bring to a boil. Add the cabbage and cook for 2 minutes. Drain the cabbage in a colander.

3. Heat a large wok over high heat. Add enough vegetable oil to come about 1½ inches up the sides of the wok, and heat it to 300°F. Add the pork and stir gently until it is pale beige, about 20 seconds. Using a wide wire-mesh strainer, transfer the pork to a colander to drain. Discard all but 3 tablespoons of the oil from the wok.

4. To begin the sauce, combine the hoisin sauce, soy sauce, rice wine, sugar, vinegar, and hot bean paste in a small bowl, and set it aside. Dissolve the cornstarch in 1 table-spoon cold water, and set it aside.

5. Return the wok with the oil to high heat. Add the scallions, leek, garlic, and chili, and stir-fry for 20 seconds. Return the pork and cabbage to the wok, and add the hoisin sauce mixture and the cornstarch mixture. Stir-fry until the sauce comes to a boil and thickens, about 20 seconds. Add the hot chili oil if using, and then the sesame oil. Serve immediately.

Vegetables

RESTAURANTS IN CHINA usually list as many vegetable dishes as meat dishes on their menu, and every Chinese meal includes at least one, if not two, vegetable dishes. Some Buddhists are vegetarian, but in China there are also many non-Buddhists who eat only vegetarian foods on the first and the fifteenth of the month in the spirit of healthful rejuvenation.

A visit to the produce section of your local Asian market will reveal many vegetables that are probably unfamiliar. Next to the recognizable bok choy, Napa cabbage, and snow peas, you will find purple-skinned taro root, leafy water spinach, flowery Chinese broccoli, wrinkled long beans, hairy melon, and the big, round winter melon. The recipes in this chapter use produce readily found both at Asian stores and in supermarkets.

COLD SALAD DISHES are not common in China. One of the most popular is the Hot and Sour Cabbage appetizer on page 58. This salad below is versatile as a side dish, salad, or appetizer, with its appealing mix of textures (crunchy, soft, and silky) and colors (red, green, yellow, and ivory). At some Chinese restaurants, Buddha's Delight is a mix of stir-fried vegetables served hot, but I prefer this version. **Makes 4 to 6 servings**

Buddha's Delight

$1\frac{1}{2}$ ounces (about 1 cup) baby bok choy or bok choy hearts

3 ounces (about $\frac{1}{3}$ cup) bean sprouts, brown tips removed

Four $\frac{1}{4}$-inch-thick slices peeled lotus root (cut crosswise)

$1\frac{1}{2}$ ounces canned gingko nuts (about $\frac{1}{4}$ cup), drained

1 cup trimmed sugar snap peas

A scant $\frac{1}{4}$ cup dried tree ears, soaked in hot tap water until softened,
    drained, and each torn in half

$\frac{1}{4}$ cup canned straw mushrooms, drained

$\frac{1}{4}$ cup dried lily buds, soaked in hot tap water until softened, drained

$\frac{1}{3}$ cup sliced water chestnuts

$\frac{1}{4}$ small red bell pepper, seeds and ribs discarded, cut into strips
    about $1\frac{1}{2}$ inches long and $\frac{1}{4}$ inch wide

2 tablespoons dark sesame oil

2 scallions, white part only, trimmed and sliced diagonally into $\frac{1}{4}$-inch pieces

6 large or 10 small garlic cloves, peeled and sliced $\frac{1}{8}$ inch thick

2 tablespoons soy sauce

1 tablespoon sugar

1 tablespoon Chinese black or balsamic vinegar

1. Bring a large saucepan of water to a boil over high heat. Add the bok choy and cook for 10 seconds. Then add the bean sprouts and lotus root, and cook for 5 seconds. Add the gingko nuts, sugar snap peas, tree ears, straw mushrooms, dried lily buds, water chestnuts, and bell pepper. Return to a boil and cook for 1 minute. Drain in a colander. Run cold water over the vegetables until they have cooled, about 3 minutes. Place the colander on a plate or bowl to catch the excess water, and refrigerate until the vegetables are well drained and chilled, at least 30 minutes.

Buddha's Delight (continued)

2. Heat a large wok over high heat. Add the sesame oil, then the scallions and garlic, and stir-fry just until the garlic is fragrant without turning brown, about 10 seconds. Transfer to a small bowl.

3. Place the chilled vegetables in a serving bowl. Add the sesame oil mixture to the vegetables. Combine the soy sauce, sugar, and vinegar in a small bowl, stirring to dissolve the sugar, and pour over the vegetables. Toss well, and serve immediately.

THE SHANGHAINESE have a particular penchant for foods with unctuous smoothness, and this dish epitomizes that beloved silky quality, with both soft bean curd and a combination of tender mushrooms. The choice of fresh mushrooms is up to you. Use whatever is available, since any mushroom will take to this simple soy and oyster sauce seasoning. A handful of peas adds a colorful green accent.

Makes 4 servings

Braised Bean Curd with Chinese Mushrooms

Vegetable oil, for passing through

8 Chinese dried black mushrooms, soaked in hot tap water until softened, stems trimmed, caps cut in half

$^1/_3$ cup canned straw mushrooms, drained and cut in half lengthwise

$^1/_3$ cup sliced fresh mushrooms

1 pound soft or silken bean curd, drained (see Note), cut in half lengthwise, and cut crosswise 5 times to get 12 pieces

1 scallion, white and green parts, trimmed and sliced diagonally into $^1/_2$-inch pieces

$1^1/_2$ cups plus 3 tablespoons Chicken Stock (page 70) or canned chicken broth

1 tablespoon rice wine or dry sherry

3 tablespoons soy sauce

1 teaspoon oyster sauce

$^1/_4$ teaspoon sugar

Pinch of ground white pepper

1 tablespoon cornstarch

1 tablespoon dark sesame oil

1. Heat a large wok over high heat. Add enough oil to come about 1 inch up the sides of the wok, and heat it to 325°F. Add the soaked mushrooms, straw mushrooms, and fresh mushrooms, and stir gently until the fresh mushrooms are soft and light brown, about 1 minute. Using a smooth metal strainer, transfer the mushrooms to a colander to drain. Carefully add the bean curd to the wok, and pan-fry, barely moving the bean curd, until it is light brown, about 30 seconds. Using a spatula, gently turn the bean curd over, one or two pieces at a time, so as to avoid breaking the pieces. Cook for

30 seconds. Using a smooth metal strainer, transfer the bean curd to a shallow, smooth colander to drain. Discard all but 2 tablespoons of the oil from the wok.

2. Return the wok with the oil to high heat. Add the scallion and stir-fry for 10 seconds. Stir in the 1½ cups stock and the rice wine. Then add the bean curd and mushrooms, and bring to a simmer. Meanwhile, mix the soy sauce, oyster sauce, sugar, and white pepper in a small bowl; add to the boiling liquid. Reduce the heat to medium-low and simmer gently, uncovered, for 3 minutes. Add the peas and cook for 30 seconds.

3. Dissolve the cornstarch in the remaining 3 tablespoons stock in a small bowl. Add to the wok and cook until the sauce thickens, about 30 seconds. Add the sesame oil, and serve immediately.

Note: Fragile silken bean curd requires gentle handling, or it will break into little messy pieces. To open a package of silken bean curd, use a sharp knife or scissors to cut through the paper on all four sides. Discard the paper, and gently tilt the package to drain off the water. Invert a plate over the top of the package, and quickly invert the package and plate together; remove the packaging. The bean curd will sit whole on the plate, ready to be cut up.

The bean curd will continue to give off water, so it must be drained again before it is cooked—just hold the bean curd and tilt the plate to drain off the water.

Choose the utensil used to remove the bean curd from the wok carefully. A shallow, smooth strainer made from fine wire mesh works well, but the typical wide wire-mesh strainer may cut into the bean curd and break it.

YOU SHOULD HAVE THIS EASY DISH in your repertoire; it's a great side dish, but can also do duty as a tasty vegetarian main course.

Makes 4 to 6 servings

Broccoli with Garlic Sauce

1 pound broccoli florets
$\frac{1}{2}$ small red bell pepper, seeds and ribs removed, cut into strips about
    $1\frac{1}{2}$ inches long and $\frac{1}{4}$ inch wide

Sauce
2 tablespoons soy sauce
2 tablespoons sugar
2 tablespoons distilled white vinegar
1 tablespoon rice wine or dry sherry
$\frac{1}{2}$ teaspoon ground white pepper
1 tablespoon cornstarch

2 tablespoons vegetable oil
2 scallions, white and green parts, trimmed and minced
1 tablespoon peeled and minced fresh ginger
6 garlic cloves, peeled and minced
1 tablespoon hot bean paste
1 teaspoon hot chili oil, optional
1 tablespoon dark sesame oil

1. Bring a large pot of water to a boil over high heat. Add the broccoli and cook until it is crisp-tender but slightly undercooked, about 1 minute. Using a wide wire-mesh strainer, transfer the broccoli to a colander. Place a plate inside the colander on top of the broccoli, and let stand to drain excess water from the broccoli. Add the bell pepper to the boiling water and cook until crisp-tender, about 1 minute. Drain the red pepper in a fine wire-mesh strainer.

2. To begin the sauce, combine the soy sauce, sugar, vinegar, rice wine, and white pepper in a small bowl, and set it aside. Dissolve the cornstarch in 3 tablespoons cold water in another small bowl, and set it aside.

3. Heat a large wok over high heat. Add the oil and heat until it is shimmering. Add the scallions, ginger, and garlic, and stir-fry until fragrant, about 10 seconds. Add the soy sauce mixture and the cornstarch mixture, and stir-fry for 10 seconds. Add the hot bean paste and stir-fry for 10 seconds. Return the broccoli and bell pepper to the wok, and stir-fry until well coated with sauce, about 10 seconds. Add the hot chili oil, if using, and stir-fry for 10 seconds. Then add the sesame oil, and serve immediately.

WHEN AN AMERICAN refers to food as "dry," it is not necessarily a compliment, but to the Sichuanese, "dry" means food that has been cooked in oil, not in a sauce. Deep-frying green beans intensifies their flavor, even if it makes them look a bit shriveled. They are then tossed in a light sauce with preserved vegetable as a seasoning—but even without the preserved vegetable, the green beans will still be excellent.   **Makes 4 servings**

Dry Sautéed Green Beans

Vegetable oil, for deep-frying
1 pound green beans, ends trimmed
2 tablespoons soy sauce
1 teaspoon sugar
$\frac{1}{4}$ teaspoon ground white pepper
$\frac{1}{4}$ cup trimmed and minced scallions, white part only
2 tablespoons Sichuan preserved vegetable, rinsed and minced (see Note)
2 garlic cloves, peeled and minced
1 teaspoon dark sesame oil

1. Heat a large wok over high heat. Add enough oil to come about $1\frac{1}{2}$ inches up the sides of the wok and heat it to 325°F. Add the green beans and fry until they are bright green and slightly shriveled, about $1\frac{1}{2}$ to 2 minutes. Using a wide wire-mesh strainer, transfer the green beans to a colander to drain. Discard all but 2 tablespoons of the oil from the wok.

2. Combine the soy sauce, sugar, and white pepper in a small bowl, and set it aside.

3. Return the wok with the oil to high heat. Add the scallions, Sichuan preserved vegetable, and garlic, and stir-fry for 20 seconds. Add the green beans and stir-fry for 1 minute. Add the soy sauce mixture and stir-fry until the beans are heated through and the sauce is almost completely evaporated, about 30 seconds. Add the sesame oil, and serve immediately.

Note: Preserved Sichuan vegetable can be stored in a plastic container in the refrigerator for up to 1 month. Or you can freeze it in a plastic bag for up to 6 months. If you cannot find it, then double the amount of scallions and garlic.

THIS SICHUAN DISH is a first cousin of Broccoli with Garlic Sauce. Soft, silky eggplant is cooked with the same piquant sauce of hot bean paste, sugar, vinegar, soy sauce, garlic, and scallions, but the amounts of hot bean paste, sugar, and vinegar are increased, making the dish notably spicier. **Makes 4 servings**

Eggplant with Garlic Sauce

4 small Japanese eggplants (about 1 pound total), trimmed
Vegetable oil, for passing through

Sauce

2 tablespoons soy sauce
3 tablespoons sugar
3 tablespoons distilled white vinegar
1 tablespoon rice wine or dry sherry
$\frac{1}{2}$ teaspoon ground white pepper
1 tablespoon cornstarch

1 scallion, white and green parts, trimmed and minced
1 tablespoon peeled and minced fresh ginger
6 garlic cloves, peeled and minced
1 tablespoon hot bean paste
1 teaspoon hot chili oil, optional
1 tablespoon dark sesame oil

1. Bring a large pot of water to a boil over high heat. Keep the water at a simmer. Line a baking sheet with paper towels and place it near the stove.

2. Using a sharp knife, lightly score the skin of the eggplants in a crosshatch pattern, with the lines about 1 inch apart. Halve or quarter the eggplants lengthwise to make sticks about $\frac{1}{2}$ inch wide. Cut the sticks into 2-inch lengths.

3. Heat a large wok over high heat. Add enough oil to come about $1\frac{1}{2}$ inches up the sides of the wok, and heat it to 325°F. Working in batches without crowding, add the eggplant to the oil and fry just until it softens but still holds its shape, about 45 seconds. Do not overcook. Using a wide wire-mesh strainer, dip the eggplant briefly in the hot water, then spread it out on the paper towels to drain. Repeat with the remaining

eggplant, wiping the strainer dry after each frying. Discard all but 2 tablespoons of the oil from the wok.

4. To begin the sauce, mix the soy sauce, sugar, vinegar, rice wine, and white pepper in a small bowl, and set it aside. Dissolve the cornstarch in 3 tablespoons cold water in another small bowl, and set it aside.

5. Return the wok with the oil to high heat. Add the scallion, ginger, and garlic, and stir-fry until fragrant, about 10 seconds. Add the hot bean paste and the soy sauce mixture, and stir-fry for 15 seconds. Add the eggplant and stir-fry until the sauce is boiling and the eggplant is hot, about 30 seconds. Add the cornstarch mixture and stir until the sauce thickens, about 10 seconds. Add the hot chili oil, if using, and stir-fry for 10 seconds. Add the sesame oil, and serve immediately.

IF YOU EVER ATTEND a traditional Chinese banquet, chances are this lovely Shanghainese dish of glossy, braised mushrooms on a bed of emerald green baby bok choy will be served. At these special occasions, it is made with the very best dried mushrooms (meaning the largest, with the most beautifully marked caps). At home, use normal-size dried mushrooms, and the results will still be excellent.

Makes 4 servings

Lily in the Wood

Vegetable oil, for passing through, plus 2 tablespoons
12 Chinese dried black mushrooms, soaked in hot tap water until softened, drained, stems trimmed, patted completely dry with paper towels
1 cup Chicken Stock (page 70) or canned chicken broth
2 teaspoons soy sauce
1 teaspoon rice wine or dry sherry
1½ teaspoons sugar
½ teaspoon oyster sauce
12 bok choy hearts or baby bok choy
2 teaspoons cornstarch
1 teaspoon dark sesame oil

1. Bring a medium saucepan of lightly salted water to a boil over high heat, and keep it at a low boil.

2. Heat a large wok over high heat. Add enough vegetable oil to come 1 inch up the sides of the wok, and heat it to 300°F. Add the mushrooms and stir gently until they are shiny and glossy with oil, about 1 minute. Using a wide wire-mesh strainer, transfer the mushrooms to a colander to drain. Discard the oil.

3. Return the wok to high heat. Mix ½ cup of the stock with the soy sauce, rice wine, 1 teaspoon of the sugar, and the oyster sauce in a small bowl. Add to the wok, and return the mushrooms to the wok. Bring to a boil. Reduce the heat to medium and simmer, uncovered, until the sauce has reduced by half, about 2 minutes.

4. While the mushrooms are simmering, prepare the bok choy: Return the saucepan of water to a boil, add the bok choy, and cook until crisp-tender, about 1½ minutes. Drain in a colander.

5. Heat another large wok or a large skillet over high heat. Add the 2 tablespoons vegetable oil and heat until shimmering. Add the bok choy and the remaining $\frac{1}{2}$ teaspoon sugar, and stir-fry for 30 seconds. Add the remaining $\frac{1}{2}$ cup chicken stock and bring to a boil.

6. Dissolve the cornstarch in 3 tablespoons cold water in a small bowl. Stir half the cornstarch mixture into the mushrooms, and stir the remaining half into the bok choy. Add the sesame oil to the mushrooms. Transfer the bok choy to a serving platter, and arrange in a circular pattern with the leafy tops in the center. Place the mushrooms in the center of the bok choy, and serve immediately.

IN SHANGHAI, the Chinese call this fast-cooking dish "Two Winters," because it was traditionally made only with the mushrooms and bamboo shoots that grew in the winter—but now, with the availability of dried mushrooms and canned bamboo shoots, it can be made year-round. Buy canned whole bamboo shoots, not sliced; and if you want the best (and the priciest), look for "winter" on the label.

This dish makes four servings when it accompanies a whole chicken, for example, but only two servings when eaten by itself with rice.   **Makes 2 to 4 servings**

Sautéed Mushrooms with Bamboo Shoots

Vegetable oil, for passing through
8 ounces (2 whole) canned bamboo shoots, cut into wedges
   1 inch long and $\frac{1}{2}$ inch at the thickest part
10 to 12 large Chinese dried black mushrooms (about 1 cup),
   soaked in hot tap water until softened, trimmed, caps cut in half
$1\frac{1}{2}$ cups Chicken Stock (page 70) or canned chicken broth
2 tablespoons soy sauce
2 tablespoons sugar
1 tablespoon distilled white vinegar
1 tablespoon cornstarch
2 teaspoons dark sesame oil

1. Heat a large wok over high heat. Add enough oil to come 1 inch up the sides of the wok, and heat it to 300°F. Add the bamboo shoots and mushrooms, and stir gently for 1 minute. Using a wide wire-mesh strainer, transfer the bamboo shoots and mushrooms to a colander to drain. Discard all but 2 tablespoons of the oil from the wok.

2. Mix the stock, soy sauce, sugar, and vinegar in a small bowl, and set it aside. Dissolve the cornstarch in 3 tablespoons cold water in another small bowl, and set it aside.

3. Return the wok with the oil to high heat. Add the bamboo shoots, mushrooms, and soy sauce mixture, and bring to a boil. Reduce the heat to medium and simmer until the sauce is reduced by half, about 4 minutes. Stir in the cornstarch mixture and cook for 20 seconds. Add the sesame oil, and serve immediately.

SINCE BEAN CURD is both inexpensive and nutritious, it is often served at family meals. This Sichuan dish, called Ma Po Bean Curd, is very popular because it is as tasty as it is inexpensive. While it sings out with the bold flavors of hot bean paste and garlic, Sichuan peppercorns are the real stars here. These unique dried berries have a strange numbing effect on the palate, even though they aren't spicy-hot. They were outlawed in this country for a few years due to the allegation that they carried a citrus blight, but they have been cleared of any wrongdoing and are now available again.

As a one-dish meal accompanied by rice, this will serve two people.

Makes 2 to 4 servings

Spicy Bean Curd

1 pound silken bean curd (see Note, page 212)
2 tablespoons vegetable oil
2 scallions, white and green parts separate, trimmed and minced
2 garlic cloves, peeled and minced
$\frac{1}{2}$ to 1 teaspoon Sichuan pepper powder or finely ground Sichuan peppercorns
$1\frac{1}{2}$ to 2 tablespoons hot bean paste
2 cups Chicken Stock (page 70) or canned chicken broth
2 Chinese dried black mushrooms, soaked in hot tap water until softened,
   stems trimmed, caps minced
1 tablespoon rice wine or dry sherry
1 teaspoon sugar
$\frac{1}{2}$ teaspoon oyster sauce
2 teaspoons soy sauce
$\frac{3}{4}$ teaspoon salt
1 tablespoon hot chili oil, optional
1 tablespoon dark sesame oil
1 tablespoon cornstarch

1. Drain the bean curd. Cut it in half horizontally, cut the halves lengthwise twice, and then cut the pieces crosswise three times to get 24 cubes (12 cubes on each layer).

2. Heat a large wok over high heat, and add the vegetable oil. Add the white part of the scallions, garlic, Sichuan pepper, and hot bean paste. Stir-fry until the scallions wilt,

about 20 seconds. Add the bean curd, stock, mushrooms, rice wine, sugar, oyster sauce, soy sauce, salt, hot chili oil, if using, and the sesame oil. Lower the heat to medium and simmer until the sauce has reduced slightly, about 2 minutes.

3. Dissolve the cornstarch in 3 tablespoons cold water in a small bowl. Add the cornstarch mixture to the wok, bring to a boil, and cook until the sauce thickens, about 30 seconds. Carefully transfer the bean curd and the sauce to a serving dish. Garnish with the scallion greens, and serve immediately.

Note: This dish is sometimes made with ground pork as an additional seasoning. In step 2, after stir-frying the scallions, add about 2 ounces ground pork and stir-fry, breaking up the meat with a spoon, until it loses its pink color, about 1½ minutes. Then add the bean curd and proceed with the recipe.

BEIJING DUCK is one of the most festive of all Chinese dishes, and when it is served at a banquet, vegetarians feel left out. This Hunan-style vegetable version is a delicious impostor: Fresh bean curd skin surrounds a filling of mushrooms and bamboo shoots, and the packet is fried until crisp, just like the Beijing duck skin. And like its meaty cousin, it is usually served with Chinese pancakes, a hoisin-based sauce, and slivered scallions and cucumbers. Here it is served with just the sauce and pancakes, but the embellishments are optional.

Makes 2 to 4 servings

Vegetable "Duck" Pie

Filling
1 tablespoon vegetable oil

$1/4$ cup (3 large) Chinese dried black mushrooms, soaked in hot tap water until softened, stems trimmed, caps minced

$1/4$ cup minced canned bamboo shoots

$1/2$ teaspoon sugar

$1/8$ teaspoon salt

Sauce
$1/2$ cup hoisin sauce

$1 1/2$ teaspoons rice wine or dry sherry

$1 1/2$ teaspoons distilled white vinegar

$1/2$ teaspoon dark sesame oil

Pie
$1/2$ teaspoon soy sauce

One 30-inch-diameter bean curd sheet

$1/4$ cup all-purpose flour

$1/2$ large egg white (beat a whole egg white until foamy and then measure out half)

Vegetable oil, for deep-frying

8 small mu shu (also called Mandarin) pancakes, about 4 inches in diameter, or 4 large mu shu pancakes, about 8 inches in diameter

1. To make the filling, heat a large wok over high heat. Add the oil and heat until shimmering. Add the mushrooms, bamboo shoots, sugar, and salt, and stir-fry until heated through, about 15 seconds. Transfer to a plate and set it aside.

2. Fill the bottom of an Asian-style steamer with an inch or two of water, and bring it to a boil over high heat. (A collapsible Western-style steamer set in a large saucepan with $\frac{1}{2}$ inch of water works well, too.) Keep the water boiling so the steamer will be ready for the pancakes.

3. To make the sauce, mix the hoisin sauce, rice wine, vinegar, and sesame oil in a small serving bowl. Set it aside.

4. To prepare the pie, mix the soy sauce with $1\frac{1}{2}$ tablespoons water in a small bowl. Place the bean curd sheet on a cutting board and fold it in half, so you have a half circle. Using your fingers, gently spread the soy sauce mixture over the sheet. Spread the filling mixture in the center of the skin. Fold the sides over, and then roll up from the bottom, so you have a closed packet that is about 8 inches long and 4 inches wide.

5. Mix the flour, egg white, and $\frac{1}{2}$ cup of water in a medium bowl. Using your fingers, a spoon, or a pastry brush, spread this batter on both sides of the vegetable pie to coat it.

6. Heat a large wok over high heat. Add enough oil to come about $1\frac{1}{2}$ inches up the sides of the wok, and heat it to 325°F. Add the pie and deep-fry, ladling oil over the top as it cooks, until the underside of the pie is golden, about $1\frac{1}{2}$ minutes. The pie should float in the oil and puff up. Turn it over and fry until the other side is golden, about $1\frac{1}{2}$ minutes. Using a wide wire strainer, carefully transfer the pie to paper towels to drain.

7. Meanwhile, place the pancakes in the steamer and cover it. Heat until the pancakes are hot, about 2 minutes.

8. Transfer the pie to a serving platter, and cut it into 8 pieces. Surround the pie with the pancakes, with the bowl of hoisin sauce on the side. Serve immediately. Let each guest spread hoisin sauce on a pancake, add a slice or two of the pie (depending on the size of the pancakes), and roll the pancake up to eat.

Noodles and Rice

*I*N CHINA, northerners traditionally eat noodles because rice doesn't grow there, whereas in the south, where rice grows easily, it is the preferred starch.

Rice is an area where we see the different food preferences between the Chinese and Westerners. The Chinese prefer soft rice, while Westerners like firmer rice. Serving brown rice with Chinese food is an American creation. To the Chinese, pristine white rice symbolizes pure food; only the poorest people ate brown rice. But no matter what your preference, there is no arguing that rice is the perfect accompaniment to all Chinese entrées.

In China leftover rice is never wasted; it is turned into fried rice, a popular lunchtime meal—it is rarely served at dinner. Every day, millions of Chinese mothers prepare lunches of fried rice made with rice and bits of other foods left over from the previous night's dinner.

Other kinds of rice include sweet (not actually sugary, but sticky and soft) rice, which is used to stuff poultry and lotus leaves, and also to make desserts. Fermented red rice is used to color and flavor other foods, but is not eaten by itself.

Noodles come fat and thin, round and flat, opaque and transparent. They are made from wheat, rice, soybeans, and mung beans, and can be boiled, sautéed, or fried. Delicious served hot or even at room temperature, they can be eaten any time of the day—for lunch, dinner, or a midnight snack.

THIS CANTONESE PEASANT DISH, with its wide ribbons of rice noodles and fast-cooked chicken, is usually eaten at lunch, along with, or instead of, dim sum. Chow Fun can also be made with beef, pork, or seafood. The noodles are cooked in chicken stock for additional flavor, but you can use water or any combination of water and stock that you like. **Makes 4 servings**

Chicken Chow Fun

One 6-ounce boneless, skinless chicken breast, cut into pieces
    $1\frac{1}{2}$ inches long, 1 inch wide, and $\frac{1}{4}$ inch thick
1 large egg white
Pinch of salt
1 tablespoon cornstarch
Vegetable oil, for passing through, plus 1 teaspoon
8 ounces wide rice noodles
6 Chinese dried black mushrooms, soaked in hot tap water until softened,
    stems trimmed, each cap sliced into 4 pieces
$\frac{2}{3}$ cup sliced water chestnuts
2 scallions, white and green parts separate, trimmed and sliced into $\frac{1}{2}$-inch pieces
2 cups (about 5 ounces) bean sprouts
2 tablespoons soy sauce
2 tablespoons oyster sauce
Pinch of ground white pepper

1. Combine the chicken, egg white, salt, cornstarch, and the 1 teaspoon vegetable oil in a medium bowl. Mix well and set aside.

2. Bring a large saucepan of water to a boil. Add the noodles, remove from the heat, and let stand until the noodles are tender, about 10 minutes. Drain in a colander.

3. Heat a large wok over high heat. Add enough oil to come 1 inch up the sides of the wok, and heat it to 300°F. Add the chicken and stir gently until it begins to turn opaque, about 30 seconds. Add the mushrooms and water chestnuts, and fry until the surface of the chicken is white, about 30 seconds more. Using a wide wire-mesh

strainer, transfer the chicken, mushrooms, and water chestnuts to a colander to drain. Discard all but 2 tablespoons of the oil from the wok.

4. Return the wok with the oil to high heat. Add the white part of the scallions, and stir-fry for 10 seconds. Add the bean sprouts and stir-fry for 20 seconds. Add the rice noodles, soy sauce, oyster sauce, chicken, mushrooms, water chestnuts, the green part of the scallions, and the white pepper. Stir-fry until heated through, about 1 minute. Serve immediately.

SOLD AS STREET FOOD, these Sichuan noodles are one of the spiciest recipes in this book, but the heat rises slowly and subtly, with a seductive fieriness about it. The dish calls for two sauces, one cold and one hot, which are mixed with the noodles at the last minute. It is best made with thin fresh or dried Chinese noodles or with fresh or dried Italian angel hair pasta or linguine.

Makes 6 servings

Dan-Dan Noodles

2 tablespoons Chinese sesame paste or peanut butter

4 tablespoons *suimi yacai* (see Note), or 2 tablespoons minced Sichuan preserved vegetable, rinsed

2 scallions, white and green parts separate, trimmed and minced

2 teaspoons finely ground Sichuan peppercorns

3 tablespoons soy sauce

1 teaspoon sugar

1 tablespoon hot chili oil

1 tablespoon Chinese black or balsamic vinegar

5 ounces ground pork

2 tablespoons peeled and minced garlic

$1/4$ cup peeled and minced red onion

2 tablespoons hot bean paste

1 tablespoon rice wine or dry sherry

Pinch of ground white pepper

1 pound thin fresh or dried Chinese egg noodles or thin Italian pasta

1 tablespoon vegetable oil

1 tablespoon dark sesame oil

$1/2$ cup Chicken Stock (page 70) or canned chicken broth

$1/4$ cup coarsely chopped salted roasted peanuts (crush in a zippered plastic bag under a rolling pin so the peanuts are not too finely chopped)

10 cilantro sprigs

1. To prepare the cold sauce, whisk the sesame paste with $1/4$ cup hot tap water in a large serving bowl until smooth. Add 2 tablespoons of the *suimi yacai* (or 1 tablespoon of the Sichuan preserved vegetable), and mix. Add half of the scallions greens, 1 teaspoon of the Sichuan peppercorns, 2 tablespoons of the soy sauce, and the sugar, hot chili oil, and vinegar. Mix well, and set the sauce aside.

2. Organize the ingredients for the hot sauce in small bowls on a tray: Place the ground pork and the remaining scallion greens in separate bowls. Mix the white part of the scallions with the garlic, red onion, hot bean paste, and the remaining *suimi yacai* and 1 teaspoon Sichuan peppercorns in a small bowl. Mix the rice wine, remaining 1 tablespoon soy sauce, and white pepper in another small bowl. Set the tray aside.

3. Bring a large pot of water to a boil over high heat. Add the noodles and cook until tender, about 3 to 8 minutes, depending on the type.

4. While the noodles are cooking, prepare the hot sauce: Heat a large wok over high heat. Place the tray of ingredients near the stove. Add the vegetable oil and heat until shimmering. Add the pork and stir-fry, breaking up the meat with a spoon, until it loses its raw look, about 30 seconds. Add the garlic mixture and stir-fry for 10 seconds. Add the rice wine mixture and stir-fry for 10 seconds more. Add the scallion greens and the sesame oil, and stir-fry for 5 seconds. Remove the wok from the heat and keep the sauce warm.

5. Bring the chicken stock to a boil in a small saucepan, and add it to the bowl with the cold sauce. Mix until blended. Drain the noodles and add them to the cold sauce. Pour the hot sauce on top of the noodles, add the peanuts, and mix. Garnish with the cilantro, and serve immediately.

Note: *Suimi yacai,* also called *suomi yaci,* is a dried vegetable that comes packaged as tiny, dark flakes. It adds smokiness to the dish, and is available at well-stocked Asian markets. Sichuan preserved vegetable is a good substitute.

IS THERE A CHINESE RESTAURANT TODAY that doesn't offer Cold Sesame Noodles? When the dish was introduced on the Shun Lee menu in 1965, Chinese sesame paste, the main ingredient, was difficult to find—so we used peanut butter, which it resembles. With the crunchy topping of bean sprouts and slivered cucumbers, these cold noodles are ideal for a summer meal. **Makes 4 servings**

Cold Sesame Noodles

8 ounces dried Chinese egg noodles or linguine
2 heaping tablespoons Chinese sesame paste or peanut butter
1 scallion, white part only, trimmed and minced
2 garlic cloves, peeled and minced
1 tablespoon soy sauce
1 tablespoon Chinese black or balsamic vinegar
1 teaspoon rice wine or dry sherry
1 teaspoon hot bean paste
1 teaspoon hot chili oil
1 teaspoon sugar
$\frac{1}{2}$ cucumber, peeled, seeded, and cut into thin 2-inch-long strips
$\frac{3}{4}$ cup bean sprouts

1. Bring a large saucepan of water to a boil over high heat. Add the noodles and cook until tender, about 3 to 8 minutes, depending on the type.

2. Meanwhile, to prepare the sauce, mix the sesame paste with 2 tablespoons of hot water in a serving bowl. Then add scallion, garlic, soy sauce, vinegar, rice wine, hot bean paste, hot chili oil, and sugar, and whisk until smooth.

3. Drain the noodles, and rinse them under cold running water until they are cold. Drain thoroughly. Add the noodles to the bowl and mix with the sauce. Garnish with the cucumber and bean sprouts, and serve immediately.

YANGZHOU, A CITY NORTH OF SHANGHAI, is famous for fried rice and fried noodles, as well as Lion's Head with Cabbage. Fried rice and fried noodles are traditionally studded with ten different ingredients, more or less. Our version is slightly scaled down, but you still get tidbits of various flavors in every bite. And there is nothing to keep you from adding more ingredients (water chestnuts, baby corn, snow peas, and sugar snap peas are a few suggestions) to reach ten ingredients if you like.

Makes 4 to 6 servings

Sausage, Shrimp, and Chicken Fried Rice

One 2-ounce Chinese sausage
3 ounces medium shrimp, peeled and deveined
2 ounces boneless, skinless chicken breast, minced with a cleaver
or heavy knife or in a food processor
2 large eggs, plus 1 large egg white (beaten)
1 teaspoon cornstarch
$\frac{1}{2}$ teaspoon plus a pinch of salt
Vegetable oil, for passing through
$\frac{1}{3}$ cup peeled and minced onion
2 scallions, white and green parts, trimmed and minced
3 tablespoons thawed frozen baby green peas
$2\frac{1}{2}$ cups cooked white rice (see page 237)
Pinch of ground white pepper

1. Fill the bottom of an Asian-style steamer with an inch or two of water, and bring it to a boil over high heat. (You can also use a collapsible Western-style steamer in a large saucepan.) Put the Chinese sausage on a plate, place the plate in the steamer, cover, and steam until the sausage is heated through, about 10 minutes. Transfer the sausage to a cutting board and slice it diagonally into $\frac{1}{2}$-inch-thick pieces.

2. Combine the shrimp, chicken, egg white, cornstarch, and the pinch of salt in a medium bowl. Mix well, and set aside.

3. Heat a large wok over high heat. Add enough oil to come 1 inch up the sides of the wok, and heat it to 300°F. Add the shrimp and chicken, and stir gently until they turn white, about 45 seconds. Using a wide wire-mesh strainer, transfer the shrimp and chicken to a colander to drain. Discard all but 4 tablespoons of the oil from the wok.

4. Return the wok with the oil to high heat, and heat until the oil is shimmering. Beat the whole eggs in a small bowl, and add to the wok. Scramble the eggs until they are quite firm and not runny, about 15 seconds. Transfer to a plate. Return the shrimp and chicken to the wok, and add the onion and the scallions. Stir-fry until the scallions soften, about 15 seconds. Add the sausage and peas, and stir-fry for 15 seconds. Add the rice, white pepper, and remaining ½ teaspoon salt, and stir-fry until the rice is piping hot, about 3 minutes. Return the eggs to the wok and stir-fry for a few seconds. Serve immediately.

Cooking Rice

White Rice: To cook white rice, bring ⅔ cup long-grain white rice, 1⅓ cups water, and ¼ teaspoon salt to a boil over high heat in a medium saucepan. Reduce the heat to low and cover the pan. Simmer until the rice is tender and the water is absorbed, about 18 minutes. Remove from the heat and let stand for 5 minutes before serving. For fried rice, cool the rice completely for at least 6 hours before using. Or cover and refrigerate it for up to 2 days. Makes about 2 cups.

Brown Rice: To cook, combine 2 cups water, ¾ cup brown rice, and ½ teaspoon salt in a medium saucepan and bring to a boil over high heat. Reduce the heat to low and cover the pan. Simmer until the rice is tender and has absorbed the water, about 45 minutes. If the water is gone before the rice is tender, add a little more boiling water (do not stir) and continue cooking. If the rice is tender but water remains in the saucepan, simply drain the rice. For fried rice, cool the cooked rice completely for at least 6 hours before using it. Or cover and refrigerate the rice for up to 2 days. Makes about 2½ cups.

THE COOKS OF FUJIAN PROVINCE are deft masters of cooking with seafood. In this recipe from Fuzhou, the province's capital, scallops, shrimp, fish, mushrooms, and asparagus, all bound with a light sauce, are served over rice.

Makes 4 to 6 servings

Seafood Fried Rice

3 ounces scallops, cut horizontally into $1/4$-inch-thick pieces

3 ounces medium shrimp, peeled, deveined, and cut in half lengthwise

3 ounces sea bass fillet, cut into pieces $1 1/2$ inches long, 1 inch wide, and $1/4$ inch thick

1 tablespoon plus 1 teaspoon cornstarch

1 large egg white

$1/2$ teaspoon plus a pinch of salt

Vegetable oil, for passing through

$1/4$ cup canned straw mushrooms, cut in half lengthwise

3 asparagus stalks, tough ends discarded, spears peeled and sliced diagonally into $1/2$-inch-thick pieces

1 large plum tomato, skinned, seeded, and diced

2 large eggs

1 scallion, white and green parts separate, trimmed and minced

2 cups cooked white rice (see page 237), cooled completely or chilled

$1/2$ cup Chicken Stock (page 70) or canned chicken broth

1 teaspoon rice wine or dry sherry

Pinch of ground white pepper

1 teaspoon dark sesame oil

1. Combine the scallops, shrimp, and sea bass with the 1 tablespoon cornstarch, the egg white, and the pinch of the salt in a bowl. Mix until blended.

2. Heat a large wok over high heat. Add enough oil to come 1 inch up the sides of the wok, and heat it to 325°F. Add the scallops, shrimp, and sea bass, and stirring gently to keep the seafood from sticking together, cook for 30 seconds. Add the mushrooms and asparagus, and fry until the surface of the seafood turns white and the asparagus is crisp-tender, about 30 seconds. Using a wide wire-mesh strainer, transfer the seafood, mushrooms, and asparagus to a colander to drain. Add the tomato to the colan-

der. (The tomato will heat slightly from contact with the cooked ingredients.) Discard all but 4 tablespoons of the oil from the wok.

3. Beat the eggs in a small bowl. Return the wok with the oil to high heat, add the eggs, and scramble until they are quite firm and not runny, about 15 seconds. Add the white part of the scallion, the cooked rice, and the remaining $\frac{1}{2}$ teaspoon salt. Stir-fry for 3 minutes. Add the scallion greens, and transfer to a serving platter. Clean and dry the wok.

4. Combine the stock, rice wine, and white pepper in a small bowl, and set it aside. Dissolve the remaining 1 teaspoon cornstarch in 2 teaspoons cold water in another small bowl, and set it aside.

5. Return the wok to high heat. Add the stock mixture and bring to a boil. Add the seafood and vegetables and stir until heated through, about 1 minute. Add the cornstarch mixture and stir until the sauce thickens, about 30 seconds. Add the sesame oil. Pour the ingredients over the rice, and serve immediately.

SOME OF SHUN LEE'S CLIENTELE think that brown rice and egg whites are healthier than white rice and egg yolks, so this dish was created to please them.

Makes 4 to 6 servings

Vegetable and Egg White Fried Brown Rice

4 tablespoons vegetable oil
4 large egg whites, beaten
$\frac{1}{3}$ cup peeled and diced onion
$1\frac{1}{3}$ cups bean sprouts
$\frac{1}{3}$ cup peeled and diced carrots
$\frac{1}{3}$ cup thawed frozen baby green peas
$\frac{1}{3}$ cup diced lettuce, such as Bibb
$\frac{1}{3}$ cup diced fresh mushrooms
$\frac{1}{3}$ cup diced canned baby corn
$\frac{1}{2}$ teaspoon salt
$2\frac{1}{2}$ cups cooked brown rice (see page 237), chilled or at room temperature
1 scallion, white and green parts trimmed and sliced into $\frac{1}{2}$-inch pieces
Pinch of ground white pepper

1. Heat a large wok over high heat. Add 2 tablespoons of the vegetable oil and heat until it shimmers. Add the egg whites and scramble until they are quite firm and not runny, about 10 to 15 seconds. Transfer the egg whites to a plate.

2. Return the wok to medium-high heat, and add the remaining 2 tablespoons oil. Add the onion and stir-fry until it is translucent, about 1 minute. Add the bean sprouts, carrots, peas, lettuce, mushrooms, baby corn, and salt. Stir-fry until the carrots are crisp-tender, about 2 minutes.

3. Add the rice, scrambled egg whites, scallion, and white pepper, and stir-fry until the rice is piping hot, about 3 minutes. Serve immediately.

THIS CHINESE-INSPIRED SINGAPOREAN DISH is wildly popular in the United States. Its charm lies in the delicate, light textures—the red ribbons of sweet bell pepper, the translucent bean sprouts, and the green of the slivered scallions against the pale yellow-tinted noodles—and the quiet surprise of the underlying spice.

Makes 4 to 6 servings

Singapore-Style Rice Noodles with Curry

4 ounces thin rice sticks (dried rice flour noodles)
3 ounces boneless, skinless chicken breast, cut into pieces
    $1\frac{1}{2}$ inches long and $\frac{1}{8}$ inch thick
3 ounces small shrimp, peeled and deveined
$\frac{1}{2}$ large egg white
1 teaspoon cornstarch
1 teaspoon plus a pinch of salt
Vegetable oil, for passing through
$\frac{1}{2}$ onion, peeled and sliced $\frac{1}{8}$ inch thick
1 scallion, white and green parts, trimmed and sliced diagonally
    into $\frac{1}{2}$-inch pieces
$\frac{1}{2}$ medium red bell pepper, seeds and ribs discarded, cut into
    very thin $1\frac{1}{2}$-inch-long strips
2 cups bean sprouts
$1\frac{1}{2}$ tablespoons curry powder
Pinch of ground white pepper
8 cilantro sprigs

1. Bring a medium saucepan of water to a boil over high heat. Add the rice sticks and remove from the heat. Let stand until the rice sticks soften, about 10 minutes. Drain them well in a colander.

2. Combine the chicken, shrimp, egg white, cornstarch, pinch of salt, and 2 teaspoons of water in a medium bowl. Mix well, and set aside.

3. Heat a large wok over high heat. Add enough oil to come 1 inch up the sides of the wok, and heat it to 300°F. Add the chicken and shrimp, and stir gently until they turn

white, about 45 seconds. Using a wide wire-mesh strainer, transfer them to a colander to drain. Discard all but 4 tablespoons of the oil from the wok.

4. Return the wok with the oil to high heat. Add the onion and scallion, and stir-fry until the onion begins to soften, about 30 seconds. Add the bell pepper and bean sprouts, and stir-fry until the pepper is crisp-tender, about 30 seconds. Return the chicken and shrimp to the wok. Add the curry powder and stir-fry until the curry gives off its fragrance, about 15 seconds. Add the rice sticks, white pepper, and remaining 1 teaspoon salt. Stir-fry until the rice sticks are piping hot, about $1\frac{1}{2}$ minutes. Garnish with the cilantro, and serve immediately.

A PILLOW OF GOLDEN PAN-FRIED NOODLES, crisp on the outside and tender within, topped with a saucy stir-fry, is one of the most wonderful Chinese dishes. To give them their special texture, the noodles are parcooked in a hot-water soak, drained, and then finished in a hot wok. Use this basic recipe as a springboard for adding your favorite ingredients. In the spirit of Yangzhou, the more the merrier.

Makes 4 to 6 servings

Yangzhou Pan-Fried Noodles

8 ounces dried thin Chinese egg noodles
4 ounces boneless, skinless chicken breast, cut into pieces 2 inches long,
    1 inch wide, and $1/8$ inch thick
3 ounces large shrimp, peeled, deveined, and sliced in half lengthwise
3 ounces boneless pork loin, cut into pieces 2 inches long,
    1 inch wide, and $1/8$ inch thick
1 large egg white
1 tablespoon cornstarch
Pinch of salt
1 cup vegetable oil

Sauce
1$1/2$ cups Chicken Stock (page 70) or canned chicken broth
2 tablespoons soy sauce
1 tablespoon rice wine or dry sherry
1 teaspoon oyster sauce
1$1/2$ teaspoons cornstarch
1 teaspoon dark sesame oil

$1/3$ cup canned sliced bamboo shoots (cut 1$1/2$ inches long and 1 inch wide)
2 ounces snow peas, trimmed
5 Chinese dried black mushrooms, soaked in hot tap water until softened,
    stems trimmed, caps cut in half
1 scallion, white and green parts, trimmed and sliced diagonally into $1/2$-inch pieces

1. Bring a large saucepan of water to a boil over high heat. Add the noodles and return to a boil. Remove the pan from the heat and let stand until the noodles are pliable but not tender, about 10 minutes. Drain well and set aside, letting the noodles dry for

at least 30 minutes. You can place a fan near them to speed the drying along. The noodles should be as dry as possible in order to fry crisply.

2. Meanwhile, combine the chicken, shrimp, pork, egg white, cornstarch, and salt in a medium bowl. Mix well, and set aside.

3. Heat a large wok over high heat. Add the 1 cup vegetable oil and heat it to 350°F. Add the noodles, shaping them into a pancake on the bottom of the wok. Fry until golden, about 2 minutes. Turn the pancake over and fry until golden, about 2 minutes. Using a wide wire-mesh strainer, transfer the noodles to paper towels to drain.

4. Add the chicken, shrimp, and pork mixture to the wok, and stir gently until the ingredients turn white, about 1 minute. Using the strainer, transfer them to a colander to drain. Discard all but 2 tablespoons of the oil from the wok.

5. To begin the sauce, mix the stock, soy sauce, rice wine, and oyster sauce in a small bowl, and set it aside. Dissolve the cornstarch in $\frac{1}{4}$ cup cold water in another small bowl, and set it aside.

6. Return the wok with the oil to high heat. Add the bamboo shoots, snow peas, mushrooms, and scallion, and stir-fry until the mushrooms soften, about 30 seconds. Add the stock mixture and bring to a boil. Return the chicken mixture to the wok and stir-fry until the meat is cooked through, about 30 seconds. Add the cornstarch mixture and cook for 20 seconds. Add the sesame oil.

7. Place the noodles on a serving platter, and pour the chicken and vegetable mixture on top. Serve immediately.

Desserts

CHINESE DESSERTS, whether sweet soups, fried pastries, or fried apples, are not made with the requisite ingredients that most Western sweets have: butter and cream. So the texture of Chinese desserts is different. A dish such as Almond "Bean Curd," for example, is a lightly sweet dish whose texture resembles real bean curd—soft but not exactly creamy.

The typical Chinese desserts in this chapter are delicious and easy to make. Serve one at a dinner party with a Chinese menu, and I guarantee that it will be a conversation piece.

THIS QUIVERY, SOFT PUDDING has the texture of bean curd, which explains its name. It is one of the most beloved of all Chinese sweets, and any Asian market will have boxes of instant mixes. Like so many things, however, nothing beats homemade. Typically, it is served with canned fruit cocktail, but the presentation is much improved with a combination of fresh fruits, like berries, plums, or peeled and sliced peaches.

We use both agar-agar and gelatin because although they appear to be similar agents, they produce different results. Gelatin makes a liquid jell, as does agar-agar. But agar-agar also gives slipperiness to the "bean curd" while at the same time allowing the "bean curd" to be cut into distinct separate pieces.

Makes 6 to 8 servings

Almond "Bean Curd"

1 envelope (2½ teaspoons) unflavored gelatin, such as Knox
1 cup sugar
¾ cup evaporated milk
½ cup sweetened condensed milk
2 tablespoons agar-agar flakes (very loosely packed)
1 tablespoon almond extract
Fresh fruit, for serving

1. Sprinkle the gelatin over ¼ cup cold water in a small bowl and let stand until the gelatin is softened, about 10 minutes.

2. Bring 5¾ cups of water to a boil in a medium saucepan over high heat. Add the sugar, softened gelatin, evaporated milk, condensed milk, agar-agar, and almond extract. Reduce the heat to medium-low and simmer, uncovered, whisking often, until the agar-agar dissolves, about 20 minutes.

3. Strain the mixture through a wire strainer into a 9 × 13-inch (3 quart) baking dish. Skim off the foam so that the surface is smooth. Cool, then cover with plastic wrap and refrigerate until set, about 3 hours. (The almond "bean curd" can be made up to 2 days ahead.)

4. Using a sharp knife, cut the pudding into pieces about ½ inch square. Spoon into serving bowls, garnish with fresh fruit, and serve chilled.

THIS DESSERT FROM NORTHERN CHINA is a study in contrasts: hot and cold, crisp and tender. Organize all of the ingredients before making this dessert, because the different steps take place in rapid succession. You can also make this with banana chunks or halved figs.

Makes 4 servings

Crispy Fried Apple

1 cup all-purpose flour
$\frac{1}{4}$ cup cornstarch
$\frac{1}{2}$ teaspoon baking powder
Vegetable oil, for deep-frying, plus 2 tablespoons, plus 1 teaspoon
1 teaspoon dark sesame oil
1 Golden Delicious apple, peeled, cored, and cut into 12 wedges
$\frac{1}{2}$ cup sugar
1 tablespoon sesame seeds

1. Stir the flour, cornstarch, baking powder, the 2 tablespoons vegetable oil, and $1\frac{2}{3}$ cups water in a bowl just until combined. Prepare a bowl of ice water. Oil a heatproof platter with the sesame oil. Place the batter, ice water, and platter near the stove.

2. Heat a wok over high heat. Add oil to come $1\frac{1}{2}$ inches up the sides of the wok, and heat it to 300°F. Dip 2 apple pieces in the batter and then add them to the oil. Fry in gently bubbling oil until the batter turns light gold, about $1\frac{1}{2}$ minutes. Using a wide wire-mesh strainer, transfer the apples to a colander to drain. Do not discard the oil.

3. Heat the remaining 1 teaspoon vegetable oil in a second wok or in a medium saucepan over medium-high heat. Add the sugar, which will become pebbly. Add 1 cup water and bring to a boil over high heat, stirring just until the syrup boils. Cook the caramel, swirling the wok or saucepan by the handle, but without stirring, until the caramel is golden brown, about 15 minutes. Remove the caramel from the heat.

4. Use a fine wire-mesh strainer to remove any bits of fried apple batter from the oil. Reheat the oil to 300°F. Return all the apples to the wok and fry until golden brown, about 5 minutes. Reheat the caramel over low heat without stirring until fluid.

5. Using a strainer, transfer the apples to a colander to drain. Oil a large metal spoon. Working with 2 pieces of apple at a time, use the spoon to place the apples in the hot syrup, coating them carefully. Lift them from the syrup, sprinkle with some sesame seeds, and transfer to the ice water for 2 seconds to harden the sugar coating. Remove the apples, shake off the excess water, and place them on the oiled platter. Serve immediately.

Acknowledgments

We want to thank the chefs of the two restaurants: At Shun Lee, Sun Do Man, Xin Rong Zhu, and Man Fong Wong. At Shun Lee Palace, Anthony Yun-Hsiang Chen, Wing Cheung Tong, and Choon Teck Tan. Together, these chefs cook all the cuisines of China brilliantly. They shared all our secrets—like frying egg white into a delicate lacy froth—in a way reminiscent of a magician pulling a rabbit from a hat. Dennis Wang, a manager at Shun Lee West, did a superb job of organizing (and translating for) the chefs, and the entire staff of both restaurants was helpful and gracious. Kenny Ng, of Chatham Imports, our wine consultant, gave generously of his time to discuss matching wines to the entrées.

Harriet Bell, our editor at William Morrow/Harper Collins, nurtured the book with enthusiasm, patience, and wit. We are delighted that Angela Miller, our wise agent, brought us together with Harriet.

Thanks to Denise Landis, who helped test and edit the recipes. Rogério Voltan made beautiful photographs, which were styled by Corinne Trang and Aelana Walker. We are also grateful to Katherine Ness, our diligent copy editor.

Finally, we appreciate the unwavering support of our families and friends, and we are especially grateful for the support of Shun Lee's customers over the past forty years.

Sources

Shopping for Asian groceries has changed enormously in the last decade. While a city's Chinatown is always a good place to purchase ingredients, there are also large Asian grocers in suburban areas, too, offering a full selection of fresh produce, meat, and seafood along with the typical selection of condiments and other non-perishables. A search on the Web or an inquiry at your local chamber of commerce should yield some information on a nearby store. Often markets that aren't exclusively Chinese, such as Korean or Filipino stores, may have an extensive selection of Chinese ingredients.

Reliable Chinese markets in Manhattan with large inventories, including kitchenware like woks, steamers, and porcelain bowls, include:

Dynasty Supermarket	Kam Man	Kam Kuo
68 Elizabeth Street	200 Mott Street	7 Mott Street
New York, NY 10013	New York, NY 10013	New York, NY 10013
(212) 966-4943	(212) 571-0330	(212) 349-3097

For high-quality seafood, including fresh shrimp:

Centre Seafood
206 Centre Street
New York, NY 10013
(212) 966-6288

You can purchase nonperishable goods online at the websites below:

www.pacificrim-gourmet.com	www.asianwok.com
www.asianfoodgrocer.com	www.uwajimaya.com

Index